SPORTS EQUIPMENT

Price Guide

"A Century of Sports Equipment from 1860–1960"

By David Bushing

© 1995 by
David Bushing

Published by

**krause
publications**

700 E. State Street • Iola, WI 54990-0001

Please call or write for our free catalog of sports publications. Our toll-free number to place an
order or obtain a free catalog is 800-258-0929 or please use our regular business telephone 715-445-
2214 for editorial comment and further information.

Library of Congress Catalog Number: 95-79728

ISBN: 0-87341-349-0

Printed in the United States of America

Dedication

Then a special thanks to my family: my wife Bernadette who has learned to live with a husband who has a surgically implanted phone in his ear, and my two daughters Treana and Nikki who miss calls from their boyfriends, all for the greater cause of baseball.

Contents

Dedication 3

Acknowledgements 5

Introduction 6

Important Notes 7

Gloves 46

Bats 98

Decal Bats 113

Catcher's Masks 123

Chest Protectors 163

Shinguards 183

Uniforms 197

Helmets 219

Other Equipment 266

Balls 286

Hockey Equipment 306

Basketball Equipment 313

Letterman Sweaters 314

Socks 320

'Unser Choe' Hauser: Home Run King of the
  Minor Leagues 325

Acknowledgements

I would like to thank the following collectors who submitted photographs and provided their expertise, without which this book would never have been possible:

Jim Griffith, John Genantonio, Joel Larson, Dan Knoll, Bill Barnhart, Mike Collins, Joe Phillips, Alan Ostrow, and Dick Hines.

THANK YOU ONE AND ALL FOR ALL YOUR EFFORTS.

Introduction

Since the beginning of time there have been sporting events, and with each event some equipment was needed. During the great crusades, people amused themselves by attending jousting events. A lot of equipment was required by the participant: a lance, helmet, protective wear, athletic supports, etc. Much like a batter needs his bat and a catcher needs his pads, or a football game needs a ball and the players need helmets. Well, you get the picture. As this country expanded after the Civil War, so too, did the team sports that we have come to love.

Hockey dates back, in some form, to the Egyptian age with the first reported hockey game played in Montreal, Canada, in 1875. Soon after it was being played at America's northern borders.

Football was played in some form during the Civil War and soon after became a popular college pastime. Baseball became the American pastime soon after the Civil War and kids have been throwing balls through hoops or baskets for ages.

As the games advanced, so did the equipment used in each sport. Gloves were introduced to baseball in the 1870s. Shinguards, already used in football, expanded into major league baseball by Giants' catcher Roger Bresnahan in 1907. Football helmets have evolved from simple leather head coverings, with little or no padding, to the helmets of today. Hockey goalies' equipment has emerged from no protection at all to the all-encompassing gear seen today. Basketball players had strange eye glass protectors that looked like a baseball mask above the nose.

As time and equipment have progressed, more and more people have come to appreciate the old equipment, sometimes out of nostalgia for a simpler time, but often for the sheer aesthetic beauty of the early gear. And every day a new collector joins this growing multitude. But what is an early spider mask worth?

And for that matter, what is a spider mask? What is the difference between reed shins and smooth-faced? When were they made? Which is more collectible and why?

And therein lies the purpose of this book: To help define the different styles and eras of equipment and to aid the collector, both novice and veteran, in pricing and identification.

Happy hunting,
David Bushing

Important Notes

Prices shown are retail prices based on what dealers or collectors might expect to sell the items for.

Wholesale or dealer buy prices generally are in the 50 percent range, more if in big demand, less if the item is quite common. Regional interest will also have a bearing on all collectible equipment prices. As always, price is always based on supply and demand. There are certain items so rare that a price guide may be tossed to the wind if someone wants a piece and the only one on the market is priced way above "book." That's free enterprise based on the principle of "how bad do you want it?"

Remember, this is a guide. Only the prospective buyer and seller can really determine the true worth of anything. The published prices are not an offer to buy or sell by the author or any other party.

You will find mentioned in almost every category "boxed items." When adding the percentage for boxed items, it is assumed that the box is in complete and decent condition. This means it may have shelf wear, a busted corner, pieces of the label missing, or some staining. It must be the original box for that item. Watch for model numbers. Adding or detracting values of boxes must be determined on an individual basis.

Deductions for child models are also marked. This may get confusing sometimes as men were smaller long ago, as were their gloves, shirts, etc. Often a child's model not only refers to size but quality. Cheap materials such as thin wire on masks, plastic backs on gloves, and other dime store manufacturing techniques are also indicative of a child's model. The buyer and seller must agree on whether or not a piece was manufactured for an adult or child, if there appears to be any question. If an item is marked junior or child, obviously that eliminates the guessing game. Try to decide whether an average-sized man could have played using this equipment and you'll usually be right.

There are also several references to boxes that feature a famous player. These are highly collectible in their own right, and depending on the player, the box may often be worth several times more than the item within. Since we do not know how many items came in picture boxes, we do not know what might turn up. Grading of a picture box will be stricter than its non-pictured counterpart. Any prices listed for boxes could probably be doubled or more if the box has a nice picture of the player and is in good condition. Again, it is the significance and era of a player, along with condition, that will determine the ultimate value.

Regarding condition, this may be of more importance on later model items than on earlier pieces in so much as a later piece might not have any collectible value unless near mint while a very good condition, early and scarce piece, might bring hundreds or thousands of dollars. But remember, the rule of thumb is condition, condition, condition. It is far easier to sell a near-mint decal bat for

$2,500 than the same bat in good condition for $500 or less. There will always be more people looking for items in great condition than items in poor condition. Even relatively common items, if in top condition, will find an eager buyer while a well-worn item, even if scarce, might go begging for a new home.

The same is true for child-size items. Most collectors do not like small kid's model equipment and will steer clear of such pieces no matter what the condition. Unless the piece is extremely scarce (such as a small size inflatable chest protector or flat top football helmet), buy full size adult models. Avoid softball or little league marked items as they are the kiss of death to most collectibles. Decorators love them because they don't know the difference nor will they pay for it. Collectors do know the difference and they generally won't pay for it either. While this may change someday, we are dealing with today and these are the general rules.

We should mention that there are numerous salesman samples that are quite small and should not be confused with child models. Usually, a salesman sample would not even fit a small child. Salesman samples are highly collectible and any nice example would have substantial value. Miniature creations of gloves, half bats, masks, and chest protectors have all surfaced. They usually predate 1920 and are highly detailed.

BUYING AND SELLING SPORTS EQUIPMENT

All collectors must face difficult decisions regarding where, when, and how to buy or sell their collectibles. The wrong decision might just cost you a lot more than experience. Since buying or selling in certain markets each have their pros and cons, I will briefly review each market.

Countless times I have heard from collectors that they don't care what something is worth because they never intend to sell it. That's fine, but sooner or later something will come up and you may want to sell a few items from your collection. Always think in terms of possible future resale, not as a means to make money, but to insure that the items you are buying are priced fairly and are of top quality. Ask yourself these questions: "If I had to sell this item, is it priced so that another collector might want to purchase it? Is it highly sought after and in nice condition?" If your answer is no, why are you buying it? If your answer is because you like it and are prepared to keep it forever, fine. But if you think that you might someday need to cash out of your collection, you'd be better off passing on such an item.

Keeping that in mind, let's evaluate the differences in markets, both from a buyer's and seller's standpoint, listing each advantage and disadvantage.

Card or Trade Shows: This is the most frequented market to buy and sell collectible sporting equipment. This category includes card shows such as the annual National Sports Convention, big antique shows such as the huge event called "Atlantique", held twice yearly at Atlantic City, and trade shows such as the Kit Young event held yearly in Hawaii. These shows offer great opportunities to meet and establish relationships with both customers and dealers. Since sports collectibles is a relatively small hobby, this networking is important both to the buyer and the seller.

Advantages to seller: This depends on whether you are set up in a booth at the show or simply walking around showing your wares. If you are in a booth, the advantage is that you will be attracting retail customers for your merchandise. If you are walking the floor, the advantage is that you can visit many dealers in their booths that might be interested in your items.

Advantages to buyer: Large groups of dealers usually mean that buyers have a large array of merchandise to choose from and if several of the dealers stock like material, there may be some competitive price wars going on, allowing the buyer to be the real winner. (**Note**: get to shows early since the best stuff doesn't usually sit on tables long.)

Disadvantages to seller: If you are set up in a booth, even at a retail level, there are only going to be so many customers walking by interested in what you are selling. Often, there will be another competitive dealer in the room and you will have to make price concessions, or the weekend may be bleak. In addition, you will be required to man your table for upwards of several days. Along with table fees, food, transportation, and parking costs, this may amount to more time and money than you may bring in. If you are walking around selling to dealers, they will want to purchase your merchandise at about half the cost of what they feel is retail value. Also, whether walking the floor or manning a booth, you will have to price your items. Customers want to know your price and most dealers will want you to give them an idea of where you are price-wise. They are not there to give free appraisals and generally do not like it when a floor seller tries to put several dealers into a mini-auction situation. If the dealers know each other, they may get together and make it impossible for you to move your items at that show. The best advice is to know what you want for any given item and if a dealer or customer is willing to pay your asking price, sell it.

Live auctions are another frequented avenue for dispersal or acquisition of items. An exciting event both for spectators and participants, it is an arena that requires one to do his/her homework prior to the event. If consigning an item, read the contract. Be sure of the minimum bid that you will accept, as well as the terms of commission that you must remit to the auction house; these fees will range anywhere from 10-25% of the sale price. In addition, you may be held liable for shipping costs as well as photography expenses. Note the terms of payment; it will probably be a month or more before you receive a check. If you plan on buying at an auction, establish a top bid and stick to it. Otherwise you may be caught up in a bidding war where the only winners will be the seller and the auction house. Also, check the buyer's premium. This is the amount tacked on to the final hammer price, usually 10-15%. Added to state and local taxes, these extra costs may well put your new purchase over the realistic price you had in mind. Figure all additional costs into your proposed top bid to establish a ceiling for yourself. Decide on the total you wish to spend that day and the order of importance for any particular piece. Nothing is worse than winning several ho-hum items, only to find yourself short of funds as the one item you have always wanted crosses the auction block at a fraction of its true market value.

If buying, try to make it to the preview. Photographs can do wonders for a piece and many auctions state that all items are sold as is. Take note of the terms of payment and possible shipping expenses. Several large auction houses do not allow same-day pickup and if you are from out of town, the shipping will be at your expense. Study your own strategies by answering questions such as: "Do I come on strong to discourage other bidders, or do I sit back and see where an item is going? Do I sit in front so others are intimidated or do I sit in back to eyeball the competition?" These techniques will come to you as you sit through a few auctions and watch others. If you've never been to a live auction, attend several and notice the bidders' behavior before bidding items.

Advantages to consigning items to a live auction: If it is one of the larger auction houses, they spend thousands of dollars on advertising. This usually attracts a large, well-heeled audience with mail bids and phone bids, as well as live bids. Television and magazine exposure also tend to build the excitement level of such an event. When two or more collectors of ample means go head-to-head over an item, the resulting price may be far beyond any sense of reason. If this is your consigned item, you might never see a price realized like this again.

Advantages to buying at live auction: If the weather or another event causes a smaller than expected turnout or if the sheer amount of merchandise is overwhelming in both quality and quantity, there may be some real bargains. Minimum bids are usually well below true market value and if you can pick up a nice piece for that price, you've got a great deal. Major auctions usually bring out the major pieces in the hobby so items that you may have only dreamed about will usually turn up for sale. This is a great avenue to add those really rare and valuable items to your collection.

A few more words of caution in regards to live auctions. Pay attention and keep your eyes open. I have watched more than one person bid on the wrong item. Allow yourself the entire day as some of the best bargains are near the end when many of the participants have already left. Prearrange payment plans since some auctions take charge cards and others don't. Most want references on personal checks while still others might put a ceiling on your total bid amount.

Phone auctions: A relatively new market in our hobby, it has become increasingly popular. Dealers put out catalogs or ads listing items for auction along with minimum bids and the buyer simply calls rather than attending in person.

Advantages to seller: Again, the benefits are almost the same as live auctions since buyers decide the ultimate price of an item.

Advantages to buyer: You don't have to fly or drive anywhere.

Disadvantages to seller: With the onslaught of numerous phone auctions, your consigned items may be lost, depending on the visibility of the auction company or dealer and where he markets his auction. Most dealers in the phone auction memorabilia business run their ads in the SCD (*Sports Collectors Digest*) published by Krause Publications. These ads range anywhere from a small ad to several pages with a pull-out-and-save format. Some will use pictures (these ads are usually much more successful) while others will not.

Disadvantages to buyer: Unlike a live auction where you can usually see where the bidding is and where it's coming from, in a phone auction you have only the word of the person on the other end of the phone line telling you what the current bid is. There is usually no live inspection of goods, either.

When bidding or selling through a phone auction, deal with established, well-known dealers with impeccable reputations. Nobody wants to be bidding against himself. Read the rules; most require preregistration and have specific rules as to times, increase amounts, etc. There are also call backs and left bids in many auctions. Call backs are exactly that, the auction company will call you back (even in the wee hours) to let you know that your highest bid has been topped; they do this to allow you the opportunity to continue to bid on an item. Left bids are executed by the auctioneer on your behalf. This is where the honesty and integrity of the dealer is most important. If you leave a left bid of $500 (this means you are willing to pay up to $500 for this item) and the top bid is yours at $50, you should get the item at $50, not $500 (your left bid), providing you've met minimum bid. Since you cannot see the items live, call ahead for descriptions before the day of the auction. Check on return privileges as well.

Classified ads: These are ads run in local or specialized hobby papers to buy or sell collectibles.

Advantages to seller: You can list your asking price and pay no commission fees, only the cost of the ad.

Disadvantages to seller: You must field phone calls and answer questions. In addition, you will need to handle all arrangements for payment and shipping, as well as possible returns.

Advantage to buyer: You can shop at home and purchase items over the phone without having to bid for them.

Disadvantages to buyer: You are purchasing sight unseen and may have to return the item. Since you are dealing with individuals, not dealers, they may not be as knowledgeable about their merchandise. Some may not agree to returns, either, since they may be one-time advertisers and not interested in establishing a good reputation.

Flea Markets: There is no real advantage to selling your collectibles at a flea market unless it's lesser condition merchandise. For the buyer, if you know what you are looking for and know your values and authenticity, you can find some real bargains in this market. Unfortunately, most flea market dealers will not refund your money the next month, even if they are still physically there. Flea markets are used by some people to pass off reproductions as authentic since there is little recourse in most cases for the buyer. There are some flea markets that enforce a customer satisfaction policy or the offending dealer may not be allowed to participate in the future, but this is an exception and not the rule. In the world of flea markets, the password is "buyer beware." If you're fairly good at spotting deals, and don't mind getting up in the dark and looking under tables with flashlights, there's almost always a treasure waiting for those that know where to look. Finding something special at a fraction of its true value is one of the most gratifying feelings derived from collecting. Rule of thumb: Everyone loves a bargain and the flea market may be just the place to find it.

Garage and estate sales: I've saved these for last because they will cost you the most time and yield the least amount of goodies. However, if you do find something, it will almost always be at a fraction of its true worth. Estate sales, while somewhat higher in price, can offer some real bargains and unlike garage sales, items for sale are not always unwanted cast-offs, but great items.

Trading: While not exactly a market, trading can be rewarding for both parties involved. It is a way for a collector to trade some unwanted merchandise for something he wants. For the dealer, he can make a profit on the piece being traded, as well as making money on the piece he's taking in trade. Rule of thumb: A dealer will not trade a great item sought by numerous collectors for something nobody wants or something that the dealer already has several examples of. Trading will also allow the collector to obtain an item that is rather expensive by using items he may have found at relatively bargain prices at a local flea market. If he is allowed $100 in trade on an item he purchased for $10, this will have cut the cost of the desired new item by $90. In this way, a collector can purchase items of value that he doesn't collect, then use that profit, either from selling or trading, to defray the costs of something he wants, thus helping to enlarge a collection for less money. Trades make the dealer happy when he trades you an item at retail, thus making a sale and his profit, and then by obtaining at wholesale an item in trade that he can again make a profit from. When a trade is amiable, everybody is happy and it works to the benefit of all.

I could describe these markets even further as to such things as size, distribution, regional differences, etc., all of which would affect market price, but to digress into the subtle nuances would require an entire book and this is not meant to be a marketing course. Suffice it to say that each avenue you pursue will yield different results and trial and error will lead to the one that best suits your needs.

HOW TO TAKE CARE OF SPORTS EQUIPMENT

One of the most asked questions is in regards to cleaning, repairing, or preserving one's prized collection. Since the materials used in bats, gloves, helmets, etc. are different, so too, are the recommended methods of care and cleaning.

Let's start this section with restoration. When is it needed? Will it hurt or improve the value? Is there such a thing as too much restoration? Can the cost of the work be realized in the selling price? Who should I send it to?

Restoration is an attempt to make a piece look as close as possible to its original condition. Restoration, in general, has become accepted in the equipment hobby if that restoration is declared at the point of sale. Often, the history doesn't follow the piece through the various owners and therein lies one of the major problems. I will offer my thoughts as to what constitutes an acceptable restoration but must emphasize that each person weigh these guidelines against their own personal needs.

Cleaning a bat, glove, or another piece of equipment is not a restoration. Removing old dirt, oil, writing (if possible) is readily accepted and expected if you wish to sell at a retail level. Adding stampings that are gone or were never there is not acceptable and in most cases would be considered forgery. Take for instance a Babe Ruth 40 bat or a Home Run Special glove. If you know the name was there but it is now no longer readable, to have it re-stamped would not be an acceptable restoration. On the other hand, a quality rebuild of an old glove, including all new piping, lining, seam repairs, etc., as long as the original stampings and face leather are left intact, would not only be acceptable to most collectors but could make an otherwise horrible conditioned but rare glove doubly attractive, both in price and desirability. Since this rebuild goes beyond the scope of cleaning or minor repairing, it must be considered a restoration.

Likewise, adding new leather to busted or rotted head pads on early catcher's masks, fixing cracks, removing old tape, applying wax or polish, filling holes, sewing tears, etc. are all improvements enhancing the value of tired pieces for collectors who might otherwise not have purchased the item due to condition. This would not be considered restoration unless it took on major replacement proportions. In summary, the main difference between restoration and enhancement would be the amount of replaced parts. At what point a job moves from one category to another depends largely on the piece and the two parties. Sometimes this line is vague, sometimes it is obvious.

The best advice is that if the piece is in nice condition, clean it up and leave it alone. If it has potential but needs TLC, go ahead and fix it up. It will almost always raise the value if the piece warrants it. On the other hand, if you have an old fifties Rawlings Playmaker that needs a total overhaul, don't spend the money unless it's worth it to you. If the repair is $40 and the glove, when fixed, is only worth $20, it's quite obvious that it is not worth the cost unless sentimental value is attached.

Baseball bats: Replacing missing pieces, such as the back or a piece of the knob, is considered restoration. Filling small nail holes with putty, repairing the crack in a handle or cleaning is considered maintenance, as far as most collectors are concerned. Jerseys are much the same. Simply cleaning or repairing small holes is considered maintenance; replacing numbers or team names is restoration. For these two items, this is the rule, not the exception.

And what are the accepted cleaning methods for various pieces of equipment that aren't in need of major restoration or work? The following is a list of common equipment items and the ways in which to beautify them.

Gloves: Clean with good liquid saddle soap and terry cloth. Afterwards, apply a good balm; this will add needed moisture. Avoid cleaning around cloth patches and any printing that may only be surface stamped, as it will wash away (along with much of its value). Simple finger relacing can usually be done at home with a tool from a shoe shop and some leather lacing. Writing on gloves must be tackled with care. Light pen will sometimes come off with four zero steel wool and saddle soap but the roughed up finish will be darker. Magic marker on gloves is usually there to stay. One of my favorite ways to hide a kid's name in marker on the back of a glove is to cut a template that will just fit around the name but with enough cardboard to cover the rest of the glove. Spray paint a few coats of flat black paint, then write the player's name/number in silver Sharpie. This looks much nicer than a kid's name. If the writing is in marker on the face or endorsed side of the glove, I would probably avoid its purchase altogether unless it was extremely rare. Gloves with marker on the face are difficult to sell at any price. Do not use leather cleaner or saddle soap on suede gloves as it will darken the glove considerably. Instead, just use a good stiff suede brush. If you are about to have a glove autographed, avoid using the balm as it will make it impossible to retain a signature. And while I'm on the subject of signatures on gloves, try to dry the area to be autographed and use a fine point Sharpie or pen. Wide tips tend to bleed, take forever to dry, and smear easily. Always try to allow time for the signature to dry before touching or throwing it in a bag where it may rub against another surface.

Bats: If the markings are stamped in, Homer Formsby furniture refinisher will remove old varnish, dirt, paint, and tape marks. If the markings are foil printed, it will remove them, along with any decals, so beware. Sometimes, just some good soap and hot water will clean bats up nicely, then just allow to air dry. For a final finish, you may apply boiled linseed oil, which will darken the bat a bit, or instead try Min Wax paste in a can for a nice polish. When polishing, beware of slivers from bat shaft and use a thick cloth. (If you have a game-used player's model bat, do not use Formsby's as it will remove ball marks, which, unlike store bats, will decrease the value.)

Masks: Lightly clean leather and apply balm. Take a good stiff brush to shine metal areas. Vigorous cleaning of head straps may result in breakage, so be gentle.

Football helmets: Clean the leather like you would a glove and apply balm. As for the hard shells, mild soap and water will suffice. Leather helmets that have been crushed can be soaked in hot water, then reformed on a fashion head or hat stand and allowed to dry. Then coat liberally with balm to avoid drying of leather or mold.

Jerseys and pants: I have had good luck soaking flannels in Woolite, then drip drying on a rack before professional pressing. Watch for color bleeding and test first. Dry cleaning is another alternative. Canvas pants can be soaked, then hand washed and left to dry before pressing.

Shinguards: Wash composition material with mild soap and a rag. Treat leather insides with balm. On canvas models, such as the reed shinguards, use a stiff brush and a clean dry terry cloth.

Balls: They should be placed in protective holders. Deflated leather footballs may have new bladders installed or stuffed with styrofoam, then relaced. (The final shape will not look as good as air filled.) Leather balm may be applied to basketballs and footballs. (Avoid, if autographed.)

All items should be stored out of direct sunlight to avoid bleaching, fading, or drying. Fabric should be kept in protective covers to avoid moth damage. Greasy fingerprints can ruin leather and many other materials, so it is best to put delicate or fragile items where they will not be handled. Given proper storage and cleaning, the items in your collection should last another 100 years. Following is a list of some firms doing work on old equipment. Write them for the costs and details of work to be performed. When getting items repaired or restored, determine the value of the item, both before and after. This will help you to decide what work should be performed. Don't be afraid to ask the repairman about costs, risks, and end results. Also, inquire about delivery dates if the item is needed for a specific event, such as a signing. If you have a rush job, ask if it can be done and tell them you need a commitment and see what they can do. Don't be afraid to ask for names of satisfied customers or references. Anyone who is proud of their work and who does an excellent job should be more than happy to provide references.

Charlie Rose Glove Repair
412 E. Campbell Ave.
Campbell, CA 95008 (904)378-8954

The Sports Doctor
404 Knoll Way
Rocky Hill, NJ 08553 (609)924-9293

The Glove Master
411 Main St.
Hobart, IN 46342 (219)942-1907

The Gloveman
2000 Warm Springs Ct.
Fremont, CA 94538 (415)490-3794

RTM Custom Bats
Jim Mainwaring
(310)374-3223
(310)674-3330

Joe Phillips
Glove Collector Newsletter/Club
(no repairs)
14057 Rolling Hills Lane
Dallas, TX 75240 (214)699-1808

DISPLAY OF
SPORTS EQUIPMENT

Once you've amassed a few pieces, the next thing you'll want to do is display them. This is where the creative side of the collector shows through. "So many things, so little space." That's the cry I hear from most collectors (myself included). So what are some of the options? Where do you find display material?

One of the best sources I've found is the big store display companies located in most major cities. Check your Yellow Pages under display and you'll probably find more than one. If you live in a rural area, find a store that sells and displays clothing or jewelry and ask them where they order their cases or stands; they will probably be more than happy to help you. Make sure you tell them why you need them. They might not help you if they think you're from another competitive store. Display companies will stock glass cases with lighting, special hangers for uniforms, shelving of every variety, torsos, heads, and entire bodies (albeit sometimes a little too stylish for older uniforms and equipment). Their catalogs also provide great ideas for displays and most will ship mail order.

You may also want to try some of the stores in your area and ask if you might purchase some of their old or discarded display fixtures. They will often give it to you just to get it out of the store.

Beautiful old wood and glass display cases from the turn of the century are frequently found at the larger flea markets, some with original advertising and often with prices lower than new chrome and glass cases. Some of these I've seen have ornate carvings and would be worthy cases for even the finest of collections. Look beyond surface condition. If the display case is intact but dirty with some broken glass, bargain a little and fix it up at home. (One word of caution, curved glass can be expensive). I have seen many collectors use the old cases along with the new, combining for a beautiful and functional display.

Travel to the larger card and memorabilia shows in your area and be on the lookout for original sporting goods displays from the various makers. I have several original Rawlings cardboard glove stands from the late 1940s in beautiful color that I obtained at bargain prices. They make great displays combined with a mint Rawlings glove from the period and nobody makes a new display that can compare with the old original items. I have found original bat racks stenciled, both of metal and wood, with the companies' names such as Spalding, H&B, Adirondack, and Hanna Bat-Rite. These will run from the hundreds into the thousands of dollars at most shows, but you might just find one at your local flea market.

Speaking of bat racks, for those on a budget, you can make one at home for under one hundred dollars, with a minimum amount of skill. Build a simple A frame (ladder type) out of four 1 x 2s. Forty-five (45 degree angle) the tops and bottoms of each and connect with hinges at top and side-mounted desk hinges to limit spread. Next you'll need a dozen three-eighths inch wooden dowels. Cut to four inch lengths, measure down the one-inch sides of the A frame and drill

Custom cabinet with shelves remodeled from bottom portion and used to display early 20th century football equipment. The glass helps keep dust from display.

Custom glass top and side coffee table. Lid is removable to give access to collection. (Warning: Do not let people place drinks on a coffee table display as spills could leak in. Also, glass tops might not be the answer for collectors with small children.)

Great idea for using common old steamer trunks. This is left open to display great collection of old gear much like those kept by players of the day. If you have an old trunk in rough shape, you could paint it the colors of a professional team and stencil on the team's name.

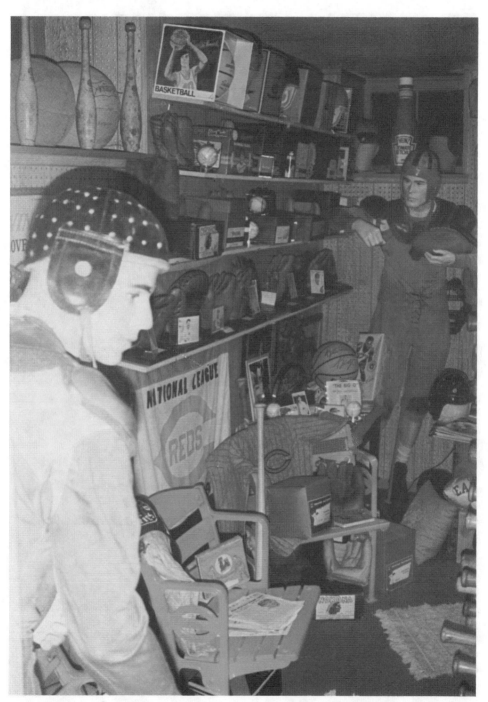

Nice collector's basement display of early equipment. Notice use of full-size mannequins to display football uniforms. This picture holds hundreds of treasures.

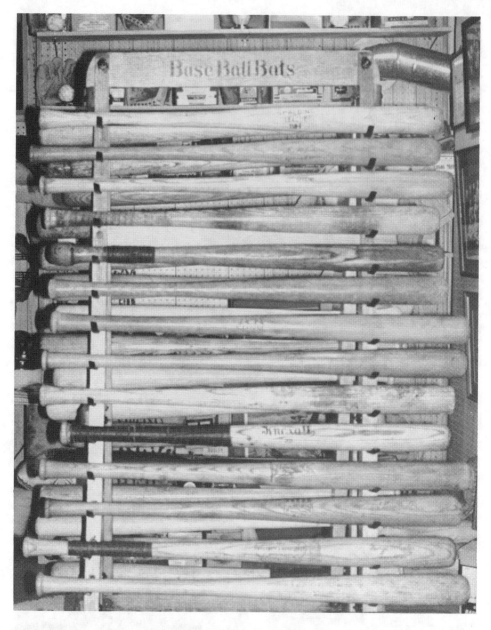

Early bat rack as used by stores during the first part of the century to sell and display bats. If originals can't be found, and they are often expensive, you can make your own for less than $100.

A nice oak and glass case made to display baseballs. Notice the holes in shelves to keep balls from rolling around.

holes. Insert cut dowels into drilled holes, after putting in a dab of wood glue. (When drilling dowel rod holes, angle your holes so the rods are tilted towards the top to keep bats from rolling off.) Now you're ready to paint or stain. If you are really handy, you can top off your rack with a hand painted wooden sign using readily available stencils.

Plexiglas cubes are easily available for balls, helmets, bats, etc., sometimes with nice wood bases, while others are all Plexiglas. They keep greasy fingers off signed items and can often be stacked to make striking displays for those with tight area constraints.

Framing is another option although custom shadow boxes, beautiful frames, and mats can get extremely expensive. On the other hand, nothing looks better than a piece you pick up that's dirty and beat up but is now cleaned and hanging on your wall in a beautiful shadow box. To top it off, you might want to look up some trophy and engraving shops in your area and have some brass plaques made. They are relatively inexpensive and add that museum touch to the shadow-boxed bat, glove, helmet, or whatever. I often have a particularly nice glove or bat framed in a shadow box with an old exhibit card, photograph, or autograph of the player. Then add the brass plaque with the player's name, years he played, team, etc., on the bottom. I've also done this same thing with a set of gloves (i.e., catcher's, baseman's mitt, fielder's) from the same era, for instance 1910-20. You could also do this with the same type of glove (i.e., catcher's) to show the evolution of the glove. These are merely suggestions. Let your own imagination design some custom displays for your own collection.

Another item you can make at home rather inexpensively is a glove tree. Similar to a hat rack, all you need is an eight foot 4x4, a dozen three-eighths inch dowel rods, and four three-foot sections of 2x4s. Notch the 2x4s to form a base similar to a Christmas tree stand with a four inch center space. Insert the 4x4 and nail the base to it. It should now stand on its own. All you have to do now is drill some holes through the 4x4 and insert the wooden dowels and cut to the length you require. Paint or stain, and hang your gloves. Again, you can make a nice sign for the top, if you wish. **Caution**: The dowel rods sticking out at eye level could hurt someone so don't use if you have little ones running around and try to place in a corner of your room where no one will get poked. That's the beauty of these tree style stands, they can hold a lot of gloves and be tucked away into a corner to save space.

Hanger stands from display companies make nice displays for your jerseys and they are easy to adjust to different heights and are lightweight. Torso forms are also available and exhibit jerseys nicely, but are a bit bulkier. Styrofoam heads make great displays for your old hats and are inexpensive and light, displaying nicely on shelves. Track lighting can be used to spotlight certain items and is classy for displays, but again, I'd like to caution you that direct light, either natural or artificial, can fade your items, especially colors and photographs. Don't put your items in rooms with lots of windows unless you have blinds. Keep the room dark unless you're in it to insure against damage. I know of some collectors that even turn their old photographs and autographs around unless someone is in the room to see them. Remember, light, fingerprints, moths, and moisture are your collectibles worst enemies. If your display is in a basement, take precautions against these elements. Spend the extra money to buy a good dehumidifier; your collection is worth it. Don't skimp when it comes to preservation. Beware of sprinkler systems in your house; if

A nice shot of an original sporting goods five-fold display and an original stadium sign. Two items that would look great in any equipment collection.

they go off accidently they may ruin your collection. I would opt for fire or smoke detectors over sprinklers in my collection room.

Since I'm in the caution mode, I should also warn you that since displays are meant to be seen, they are also likely to be seen by the wrong persons. ADT offered an in-home alarm system for a $200 installation fee and a $20-a-month monitoring service. This also lowered our insurance a bit. Weigh the value of your collection and give security a thought. In addition, it is wise to inventory your collection and photograph as much of it as possible. Keep this somewhere outside your house. (It wouldn't do you much good if it burned with the items pictured.) Talk to your insurance agent and get a special rider for valuable collections. If you think your collection warrants an appraisal, get one. While it may cost upwards of a few hundred dollars, it might be worth it if your collection is sizable. Be sure to get an appraisal from a firm recognized as experts in the field and one that will satisfy the insurance company. Read all the fine print of the policy and get it in writing. It might not be a bad idea for you to have your

This is a nice full-size mannequin used to display the gear of a turn of the century catcher. Included is a quilted chest protector, smooth shinguards, and an early spider mask. (Try some local stores that might be throwing out old mannequins.)

Nicely made hat tree used to display several early styles of football helmets. Can you spot the flat top, aviator style, strap helmet, and noseguard?

Brooklyn Dodger display at the Hall of Fame with a jacket, two home jerseys, bats, shoes, hat, and a pennant. Nice arrangement for team collector. (Courtesy of The National Baseball Hall of Fame and Museum, Cooperstown, New York)

lawyer check out the details of the policy as well. This might sound like a lot of trouble but if your collection is valuable and it is lost or stolen, all the preparation will have been worth it. In addition, a well inventoried stock and good photographs will aid in finding your merchandise, if stolen. It's a shame to have to discuss these things when talking about displaying your items but until this is a perfect world, the old saying "better safe than sorry" still applies.

Another major question or problem that seems to plague some equipment collectors is that with so much wood and leather, the collection can look rather uneventful or colorless. This is particularly true for those that collect only gloves or bats, since they can and do tend to all look alike. Demonstrate your flair for display by adding color; use old pennants and framed color advertisements from old equipment ads. Round out your equipment collection with some colorful boxes or photographs. Remember that a collection of only one type of item and nothing else can be boring.

For great ideas, try to get to the Baseball Hall of Fame in Cooperstown, New York. It will inspire you, as well as leave you in awe. Lots of major cities have museums that include sports displays: St. Louis has a nice museum at Busch Stadium and Chicago has the Italian American Hall of Fame.

If you collect football memorabilia, there's the Hall of Fame in Canton, Ohio. The Hockey Hall of Fame has opened in Toronto, Canada, and there's the Basketball Hall of Fame in Springfield, Massachusetts, as well. Even little towns have displays at local museums or libraries, featuring local sports heroes of the past. Check your local Yellow Pages and get out and see some displays. Some do allow cameras, but be sure to ask.

When it's all said and done, use your items, your ideas, and your space to create a display that is distinctly you. If your collection is larger than your display area, one alternative is to rotate the display. My office is rather small so I rotate items on a monthly basis. This allows me to sit and admire items in my collection for a month, then replace them with something else. I love changing the room a bit and I rediscover items all over again when plowing through my boxes. In addition, visitors get a kick out of visiting each month to see what new treasures I've got on the walls. Sure, it would be great to have a huge room with built-in glass cases large enough to display everything at once, but you have to

Nice Hall of Fame Cardinals collection featuring many game-used pieces of equipment, along with balls and awards. (Courtesy of The National Baseball Hall of Fame and Museum, Cooperstown, New York)

deal with what you have. I have friends whose wives love the old stuff, and consequently, they have their stuff displayed throughout their homes. I know of one collector who bought the house next door to store and display his collection.

My wife, on the other hand, doesn't feel the same affinity as I do towards an old baseball bat and glove hanging over the fireplace. If a print by Picasso or Matisse is preferred over a George Sisler bat in your household, I can relate. This is why no two collections or displays are alike because each and every collector, collection, and circumstance is different. Every collector can make use of any available space and make it appealing.

So go ahead, get that great stuff out of the closet and out from under the bed. Spruce it up and hang it up. There's got to be somebody around who'd appreciate it as much as you do. You owe it to them to put it where it can be seen.

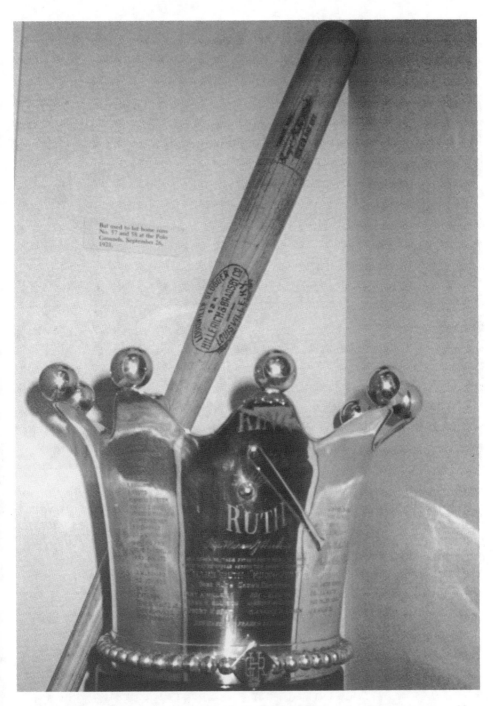

A Babe Ruth display at the Baseball Hall of Fame in Cooperstown, New York. Included is a game-used bat and an award. (Courtesy of The National Baseball Hall of Fame and Museum, Cooperstown, New York)

Hall of Fame display showing button down collar jersey worn by Hall of Famer Buck Ewing while he was with the Reds in late 1890s. The display is rounded out with an award, an autographed ball, and some plates with his picture on them. (Courtesy of The National Baseball Hall of Fame and Museum, Cooperstown, New York)

Above Left: Hall of Fame Pirates display. (Courtesy of The National Baseball Hall of Fame and Museum, Cooperstown, New York)

Below Right: Nice Hall of Fame display showing mid-19th century presentation baseballs with inscriptions, a presentation silver adorned bat, and some vintage programs. (Courtesy of The National Baseball Hall of Fame and Museum, Cooperstown, New York)

Right: A nice 1871 decal presentation bat and a striped 1870s bat at the Hall of Fame. (Courtesy of The National Baseball Hall of Fame and Museum, Cooperstown, New York)

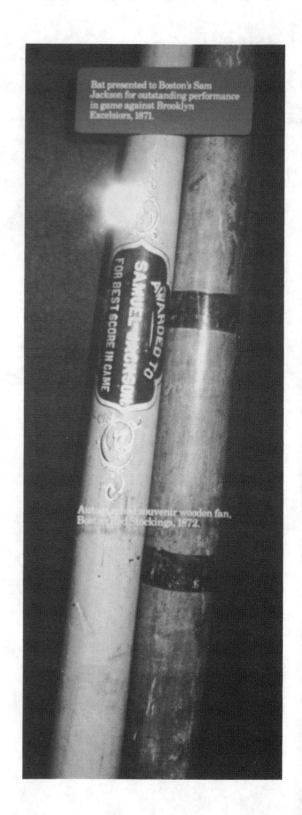

Hall of Fame display with an early solid web glove worn by John McGraw, surrounded by some early loving cups and an 1894 championship scarf with the likeness of each player. (Courtesy of The National Baseball Hall of Fame and Museum, Cooperstown, New York)

Hall of Fame Edd Roush display features hat, bat, and sliding pads. (Courtesy of The National Baseball Hall of Fame and Museum, Cooperstown, New York)

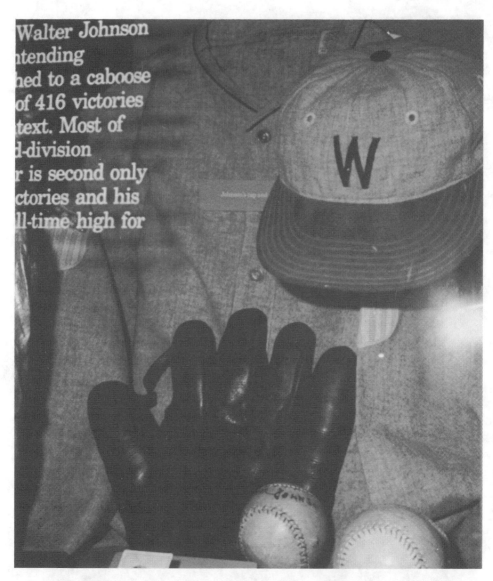

Walter Johnson
tending
hed to a caboose
of 416 victories
text. Most of
d-division
r is second only
ctories and his
ll-time high for

Hall of Fame display with Walter Johnson's hat, jersey, glove, and some autographed baseballs. Notice thinned web on glove. (Courtesy of The National Baseball Hall of Fame and Museum, Cooperstown, New York)

Hall of Fame display showing early New York Giants tour jersey with cadet collar. (Courtesy of The National Baseball Hall of Fame and Museum, Cooperstown, New York)

Hall of Fame evolution of catchers' masks display that includes nice pictures of players using early equipment. (Courtesy of The National Baseball Hall of Fame and Museum, Cooperstown, New York)

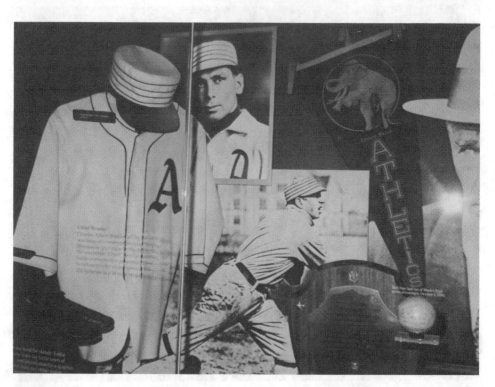

Hall of Fame display showing Sam Crawford's World Tour uniform with nice two-tone shirt collar style dating to 1913-14. (Courtesy of The National Baseball Hall of Fame and Museum, Cooperstown, New York)

Hall of Fame Athletics display features the famous early pill-box style of cap and assorted memorabilia. (Courtesy of The National Baseball Hall of Fame and Museum, Cooperstown, New York)

A nice Hall of Fame Giants display mixing jerseys with pictures and assorted awards. (Courtesy of The National Baseball Hall of Fame and Museum, Cooperstown, New York)

Hall of Fame display of Ray Schalk. It includes his 1917 White Sox home flannel as well as his small-billed cap and awards. This is one of the most stunning uniforms ever made.

Above and Following Page: Hall of Fame Negro League display with jerseys, hats, gloves, and poster. In doing your own displays, you will enhance them immensely by adding color, photographs, etc., to round out the case, making it more visually stimulating. (Courtesy of The National Baseball Hall of Fame and Museum, Cooperstown, New York)

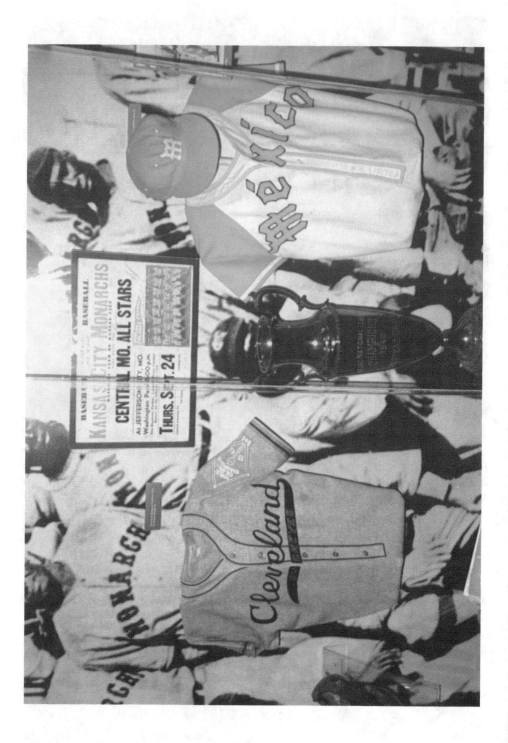

Hall of Fame Red Sox display has rare Tris Speaker decal bat in beautiful condition with handle plastered in wine labels. Also notice the burn or heat treated bat at bottom, the idea that heating a bat in spots would harden it, ca. pre-1920. (Courtesy of The National Baseball Hall of Fame and Museum, Cooperstown, New York)

Hall of Fame display with great old batting trophy and assorted memorabilia. Early figural trophies such as this one, no matter who won them, are quite rare and valuable running upwards of $1,500. Watch for broken appendages that have been soldered, as this will depreciate value. (Courtesy of The National Baseball Hall of Fame and Museum, Cooperstown, New York)

BASEBALL
EQUIPMENT

Gloves
Bats
Other Epuipment:
    Decal Bats
    Catcher's Masks
    Chest Protectors
    Shinguards
    Uniforms

GLOVES

Albert Goodwill Spalding penned a book titled *Base Ball, America's National Game* in 1911. It has been revised, re-edited, and reissued many times but it remains to this day one of the most definitive works on the game's beginnings. Nobody did more to promote the game of baseball, and more importantly for this book, to promote the manufacture and improvement of sports equipment, than did the founder of Spalding Sporting Goods, Al Spalding.

In his chronological order of events surrounding the early beginnings of baseball, Spalding writes that it was in 1875 that the first glove or mitt was ever worn in organized baseball. He credits Charles Waite, first baseman of Boston, and then he credits himself with improving "on this innovation, adding padding to save a bruised hand. The ensuing demand for padded gloves soon was being supplied by the Spalding Sporting Goods Co."

Credit for the invention of the catcher's mitt, according to a letter written by himself offering affidavits and witnesses to the event, was Joseph Gunson, a catcher for the Kansas City Blues in 1888. Apparently, he and a fellow named Decker, a catcher for Chicago, designed the glove without wire, while another man, Ted Kennedy, having learned of the mitt from Gunson, beat them to the punch with a patented and wire-enforced catcher's mitt that he claimed as his own. In any event, gloves and mitts were here to stay.

They have now become one of the most collected of old sports equipment. Much like baseball cards, it is the players whose endorsement appears on the glove that set most of the collectible value, at least until recently. While there has already been much written on gloves bearing the endorsements of famous players and their values, little has been written and nothing exists in the way of pricing on the early and non-endorsed gloves and mitts. Fingerless gloves, resembling handball gloves with the fingers cut out, are highly sought and rarely offered for sale. In addition, there has been a huge increase in the demand for early examples of the baseball glove. Endorsements of famous players, found stamped on their model gloves, really didn't come into vogue until the time of World War I or just prior. Before that, gloves and mitts usually bore only the maker's name and sometimes a model or patent number.

Gloves predating the turn of the century bear little resemblance to those worn by today's players. In addition, there were all sorts of experimental designs, some successful, others short-lived. Following is an attempt to catalog the distinctly different styles and their pricing structure. Bear in mind that so few nineteenth century gloves turn up, prices on the scarce models are truly subjective.

Front cover of the A.G. Spalding & Brothers Spring/Summer Sports Catalog, 1904.

THE

Reach Special
REG. U.S. PAT. OFF.

PROFESSIONAL

FIELDERS' GLOVES

**THE
HIGHEST
QUALITY**

FIELDERS' GLOVES

No. OB Each **$3.00**

**Drab Buckskin
Felt Lined**

Made in all sizes. We carry in stock at all times, sizes 13, 14, 15, 16. Packed one in a box. Made in rights and lefts.

No. O1   Each $3.00

**BLACK CALFSKIN
FELT LINED**

These Gloves were originated and designed by us seven years ago and are now being used by all the professional players throughout the country. They have numerous advantages over the other models, but the principal one is in the formation of the deep pocket. This effect is gained by the arrangement of the padding on the inside of the glove. The little finger is made larger and more heavily padded; this makes a wider and more practical glove, enabling the player to field the ball to better advantage, insuring a glove that will prove satisfactory in every way.

No. O2   Each $3.00
Brown Calfskin, Leather Lined

We use only the **highest quality of leather, felt** and other materials in their construction. Only the most skillful operators in our employ make these gloves. This season we are making them in three styles, **Drab Buckskin, Felt Lined, Black Calfskin, Felt Lined** and **Brown Calfskin, Leather Lined.**

We buy such large quantities of Leather, Felt, Thread and other Materials, that Tanners and Manufacturers finish the goods we buy from them especially according to our wishes and ideas. This is an advantage no other maker of Sporting Goods has.

Raw Material, Such as We Use, Cannot be Bought in the Open Market.

11

Fielders' Gloves for sale in the A.J. Reach Company 1909 Season Catalog.

48

Glossary

Mitt - Has no outward separation of fingers on face or catching side of leather. A baseman's mitt, or a catcher's mitt. Early in the century and before, infielders also used mitts. Delineation of fingers is often found on back.

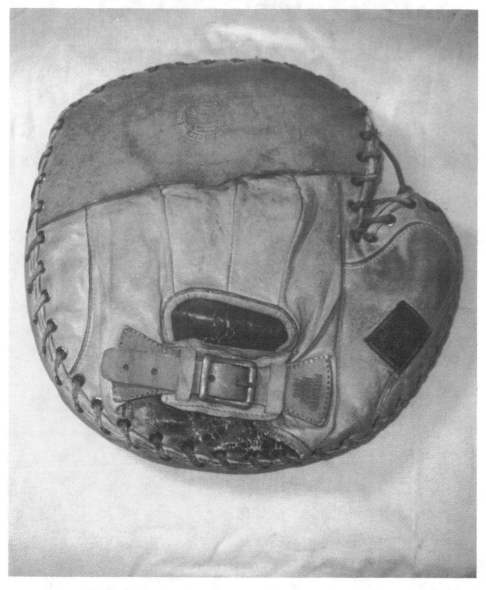

Back view of Goldsmith catcher's mitt ca. 1910-20 with Decker patent.

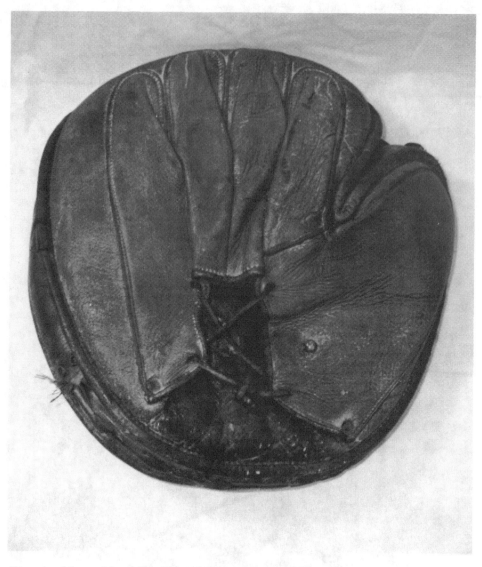

Diamond brand lace-back catcher's mitt ca. 1890s.

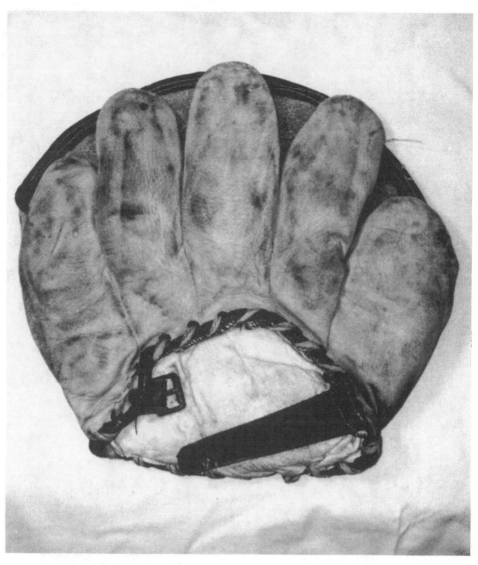

Strange "pita pocket" mitt ca. 1900. Sewn-in pocket holds at least five baseballs. Practice glove?

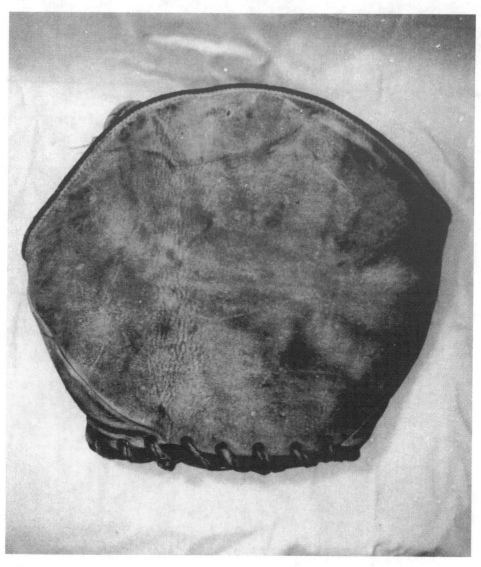

Face of "pita pocket" mitt.

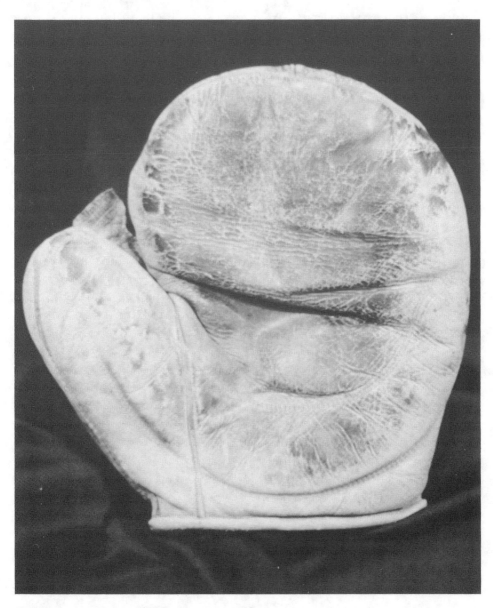

Baseman's mitt ca. 1890s.

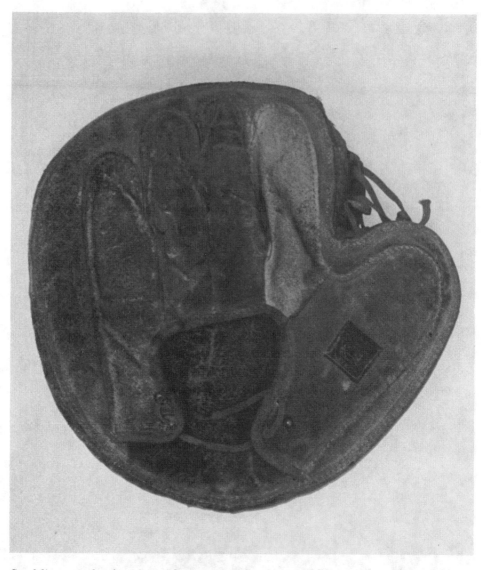

Spalding catcher's mitt with grommet back ca. 1890s.

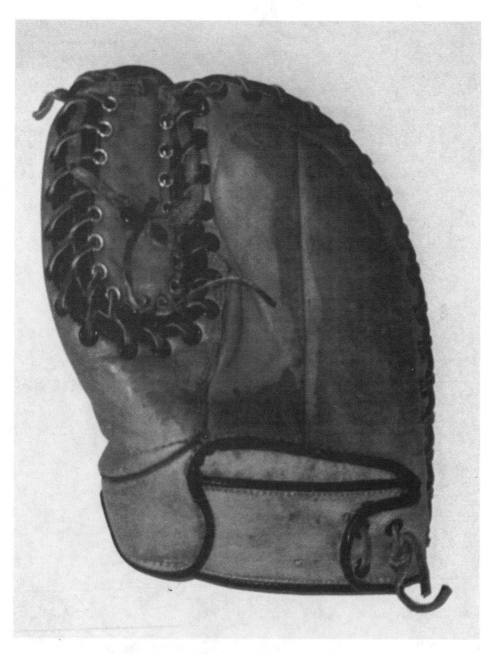

Back view of Trapper style baseman's mitt ca. 1940.

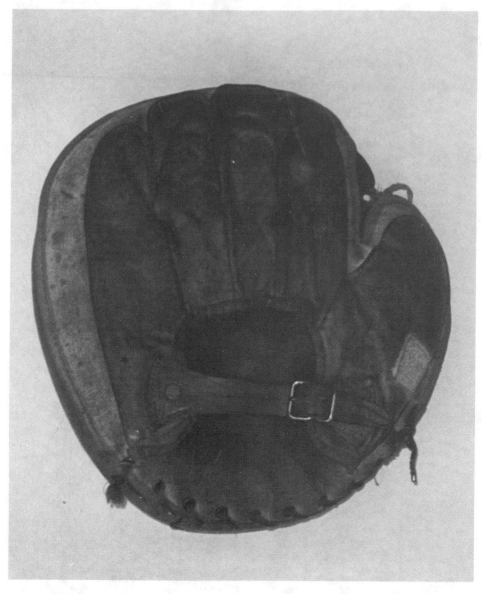

Back view of Spalding catcher's mitt ca. 1900.

Glove - This is the counterpart to the mitt and is the style used by fielders and pitchers. It has the individual fingers plus the thumb. It can have as few as two fingers or as many as five. The thumb is not counted as a finger except in six-finger models.

Reach fielder's glove ca. 1905-10 (Notice asbestos lining).

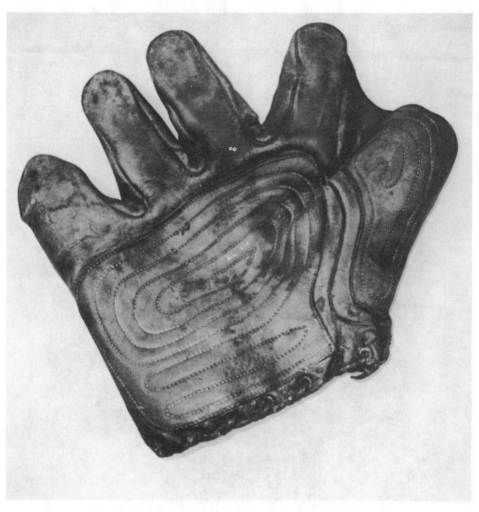

Stitched palm glove ca. 1900.

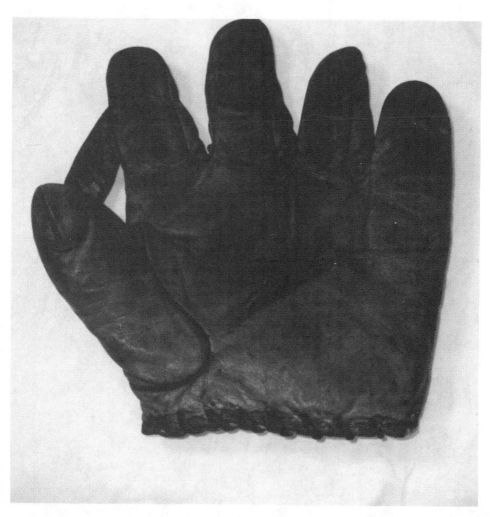

Typical fielder's glove ca. 1910-20.

D & M fielder's glove ca. 1920s.

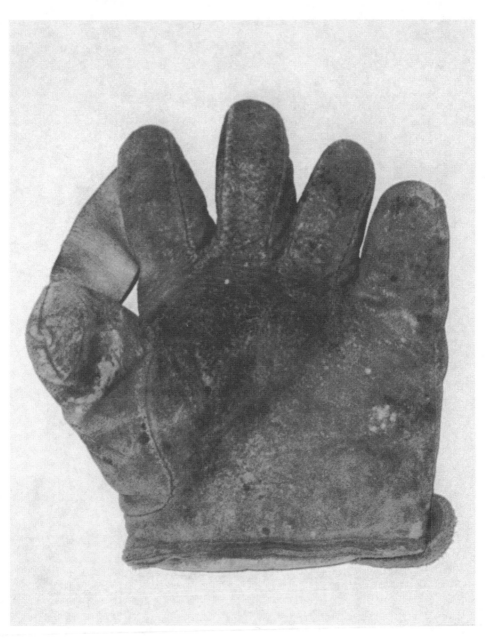

Fielder's glove ca. 1905.

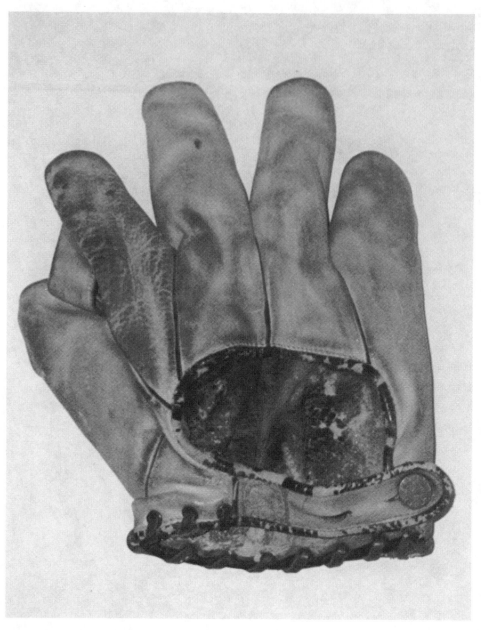

Spalding fielder's glove ca. 1910.

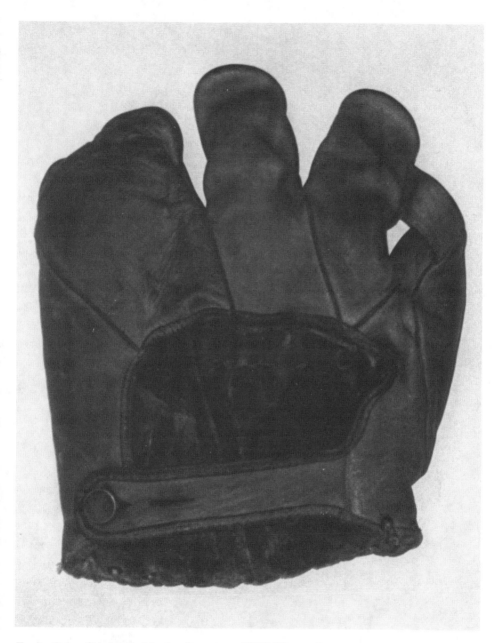

Early three-finger fielder's glove ca. 1920-30.

Front view of early three-finger glove ca. 1920-30.

Back view of Reach fielder's glove ca. 1905.

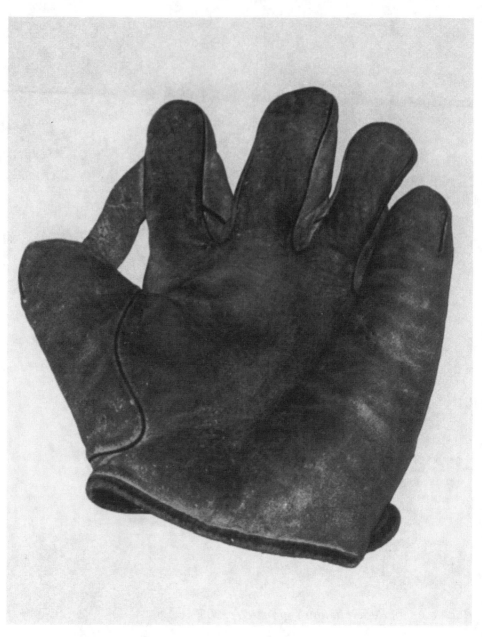

Fielder's glove ca. 1910-20.

Web - This is the section of a mitt or glove that connects the thumb to the rest of the leather. Webs first appeared on fielders' gloves around the turn of the century. They didn't really become common on catcher's mitts until the 1950s; prior to that time only a rawhide lace served as a web. Baseman's mitts used the rawhide lace as a web much like the early catcher's mitts. Rawlings revolutionized the baseman's mitt when they added a piece of leather between the thumb and body in 1941 resembling a place for a finger. They called it their trapper model. That became the standard from then on.

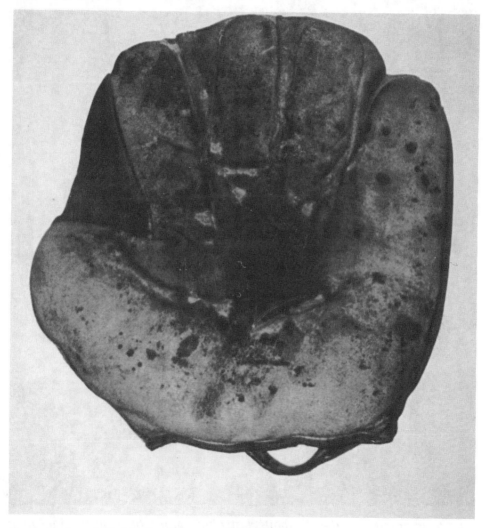

Rare duck web fielder's glove ca. 1890-05.

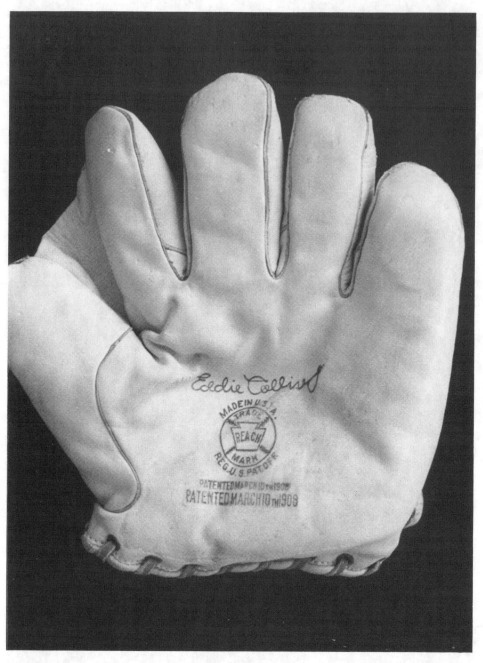

Superb example of full-web white horsehide glove bearing the facsimile signature of Hall of Famer Eddie Collins.

Fingers - Three finger, six finger, two finger, etc. Refers to the amount of finger positions on a mitt or glove. As mentioned earlier, the thumb is never counted as a finger except in the case of the trapeze style fielders' gloves, a glove in which a finger-style piece of leather is inserted between the web giving the impression that a finger might be placed there. These are referred to as six fingers and the thumb is counted in the total.

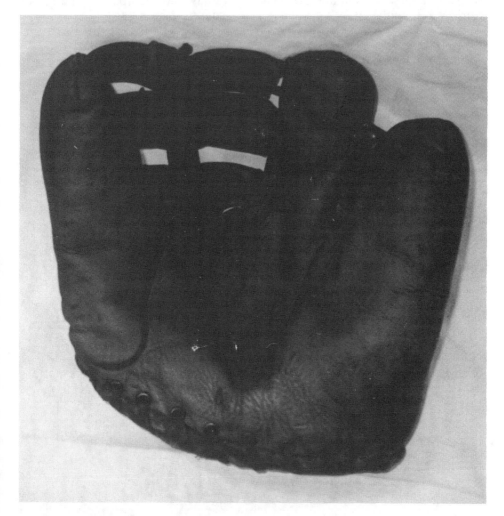

Two-finger glove ca. late 1940s.

Laced fingers - Refers to the fingers on a fielder's glove. They were laced together intermittently prior to the mid 1940s. After that, laced fingers on fielders' gloves became the norm. A single lace was standard throughout the forties and fifties. Double laced and x patterns became popular in the sixties and later.

Split finger - The opposite of the laced fingers. Again, this refers to fielders' gloves and is also referred to as a prewar style, regardless of the date of manufacture.

Break action - The cut and lacing at the bottom face of a catcher's mitt, added in the late 1940s to aid the catcher in closing his mitt around the ball.

Buckle back - Refers to the metal buckle used on the wrist straps of prewar gloves to adjust tension and size. They generally became obsolete during the World War II, replaced by a system of laces, snaps, or buttons.

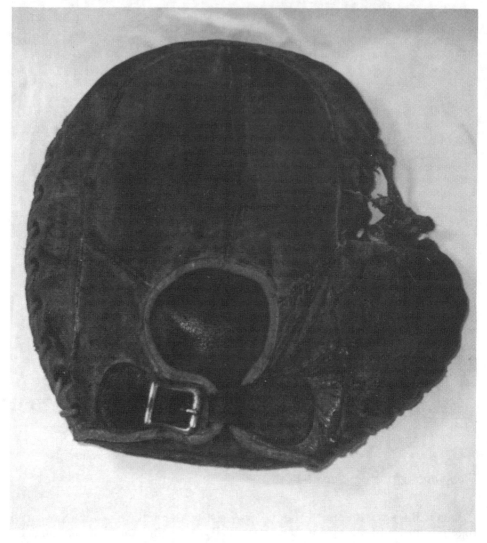

Typical buckle back baseman's mitt ca. 1920s.

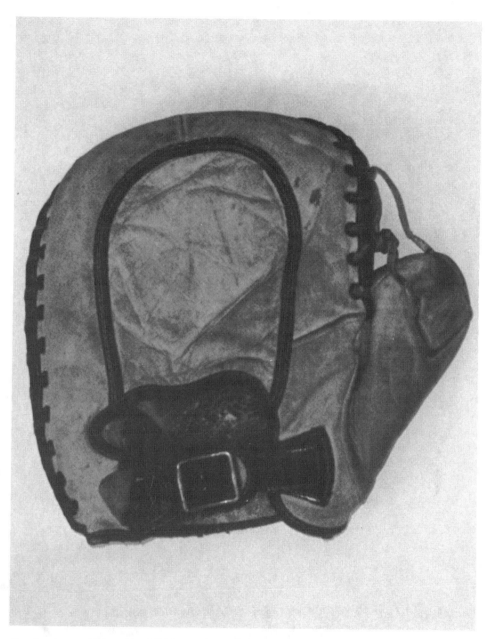

Back view of nice buckle back first baseman's mitt ca. 1920-30.

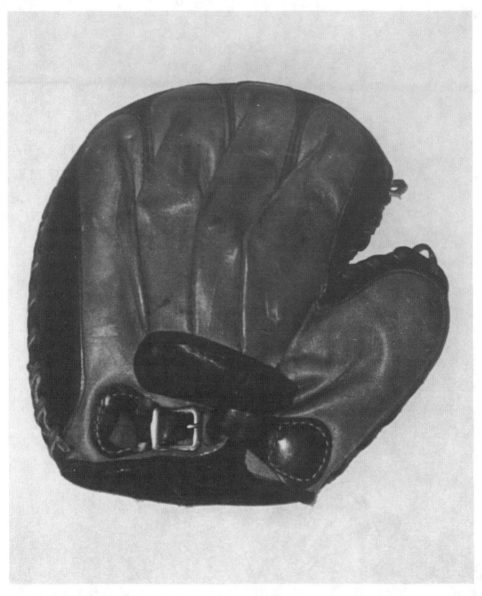

Back view of ca. 1920-30s buckle back first baseman's mitt.

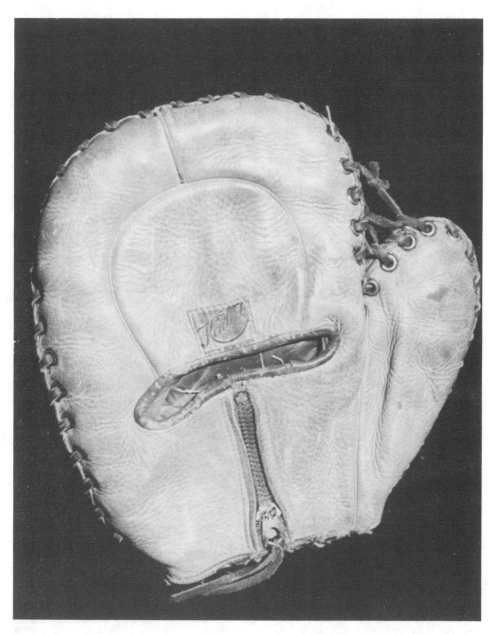

Back view of Lou Gehrig, Ken Wel mitt showing unusual zipper adjustment.

Front or face view of rare Lou Gehrig, Ken Wel first baseman's mitt ca. 1930. Extremely rare and valuable.

Zipper back - Made popular by Ken Wel and most famous in the Lou Gehrig baseman's mitt and the Muddy Ruel catcher's mitt. Used to snug the mitt to the hand.

Zipper bottom - A zipper installed at the base of the inside face or heel of glove to add more padding at will. Generally found only on prewar, split finger fielder's gloves.

Duck web glove - This is an earlier glove, usually pre-1920, that has a full web (from the finger tip to the base of a finger) sewn between every finger and the thumb. A strange and rare glove.

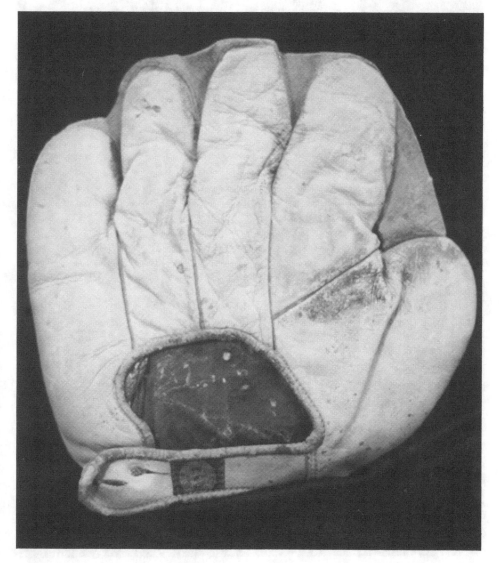

Back of thick "duck" web glove ca. 1890-05.

Crescent pad - A raised strip of padding usually at the base of the glove or mitt. It will be found on both gloves and mitts. It is usually seen on models pre-dating 1910. They were also used on softball gloves and mitts well into the 1940s and 1950s. It is usually quite easy to tell a softball glove, even if not marked softball. The style of glove gives them away as being of a much later date of manufacture.

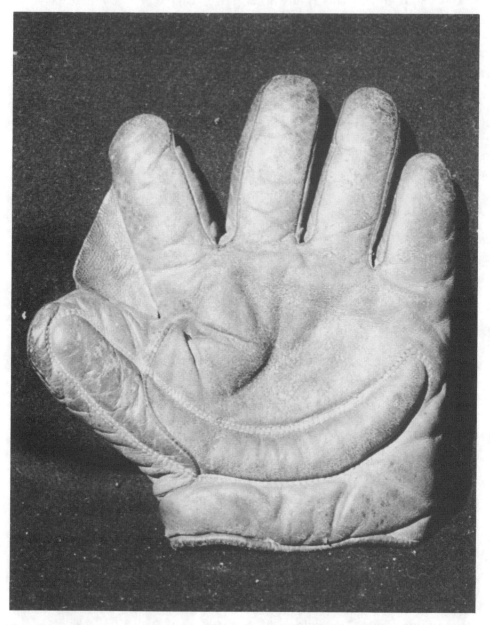

Superb example of early full web crescent heel glove ca. 1905

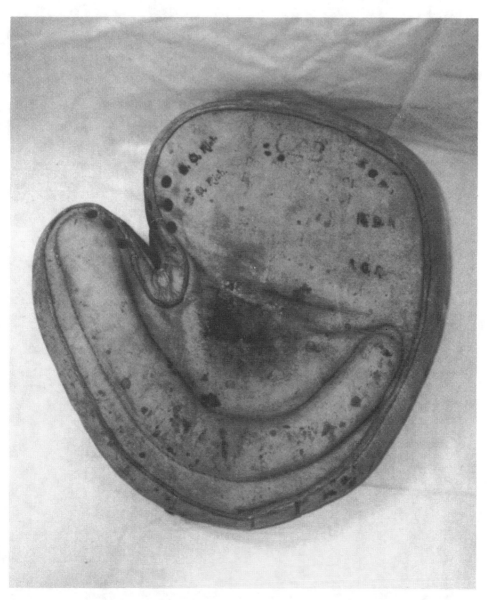

Crescent pad catcher's mitt ca. 1895-05.

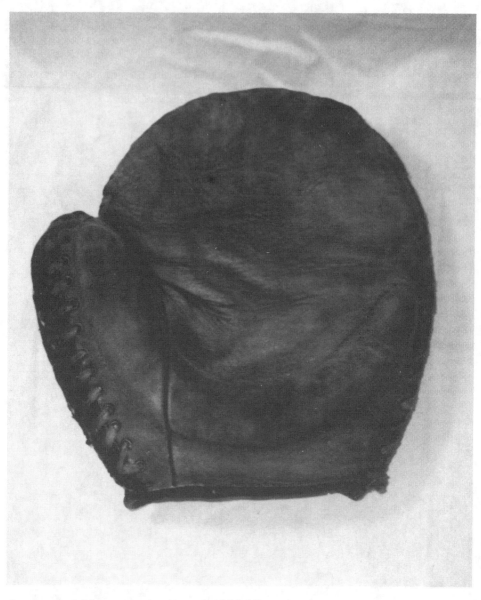

Crescent pad baseman's mitt ca. 1890-05.

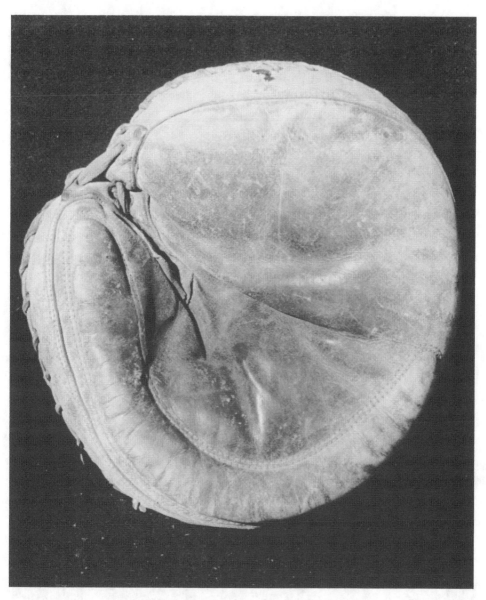

Nice example of crescent pad catcher's mitt ca. 1905

Workman glove (same as Workman's glove) - This is a style of glove that is no larger than a man's hand. First offered in the 1880s without any web at all. Usually has a metal grommet or button on the back with a string lacing system to tighten to hand. Popular from the 1880s-1900. These gloves were worn for all positions. Webs were added in the late 1880s and early 1890s, but the style of glove remained the same. The web-less variety is more valuable.

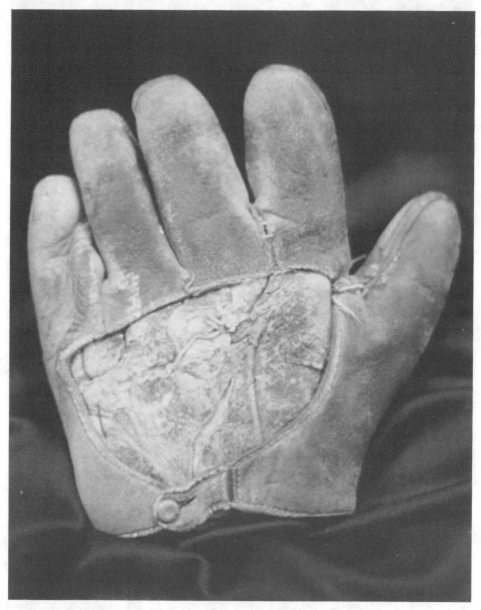

Back of non-web workman's glove ca. 1880-90.

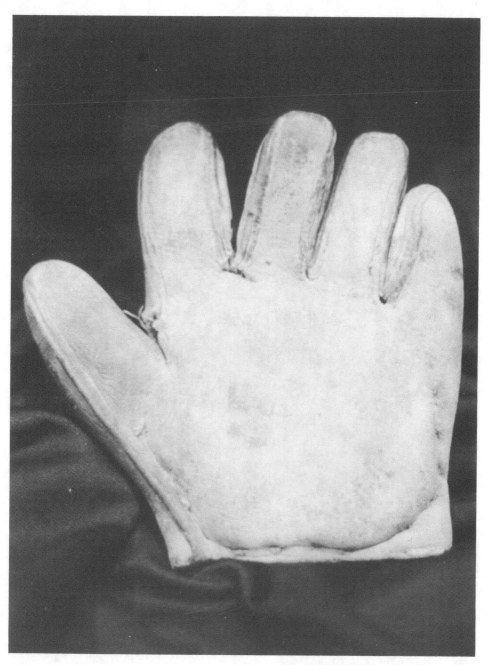

Front view of non-web workman's glove ca. 1880-90.

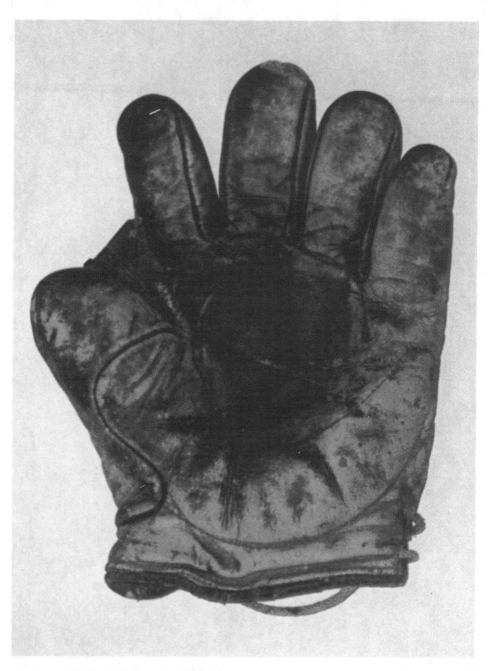

Web workman's glove ca. 1880-90.

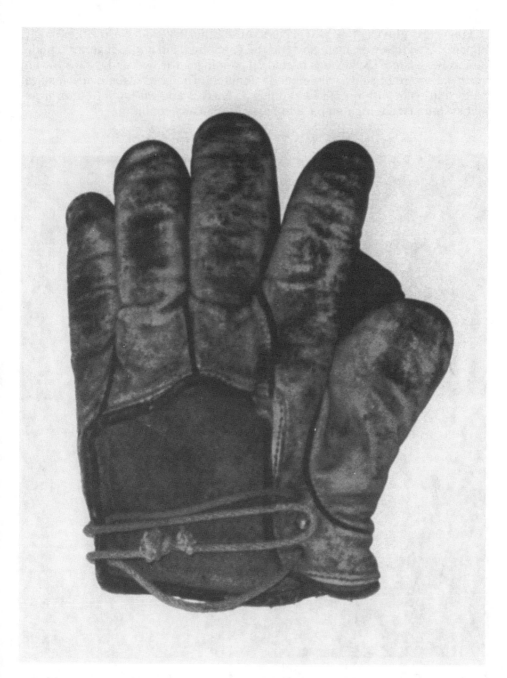

Back view of web workman's glove ca. 1880-90.

Fingerless gloves - Used by players during the 1880-90s. Worn either singly, in pairs, or with a workman glove on the catching hand and a fingerless model on throwing hand. Usually has beefed up padding in the heel and is sans the fingertips. Beware of similar style handball mitts. (The latter usually has a spiral pattern in palm with no raised padding at heel). Made with a button or grommet system used to tighten back to hand. Rare in any condition.

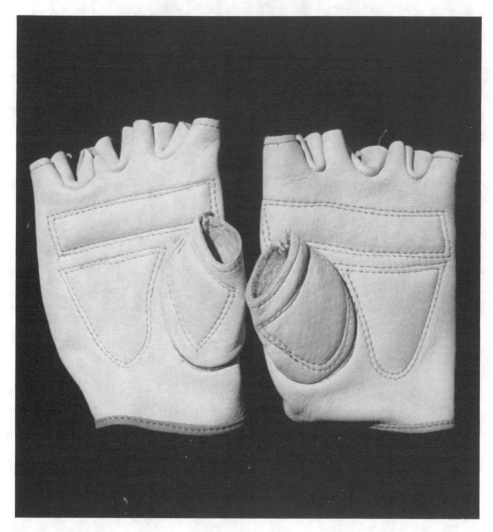

Example of custom made modern reproductions of fingerless gloves made for players that put on exhibition games of 1880s baseball, using original style equipment and rules.

Pair of Spalding fingerless gloves ca. 1880-90.

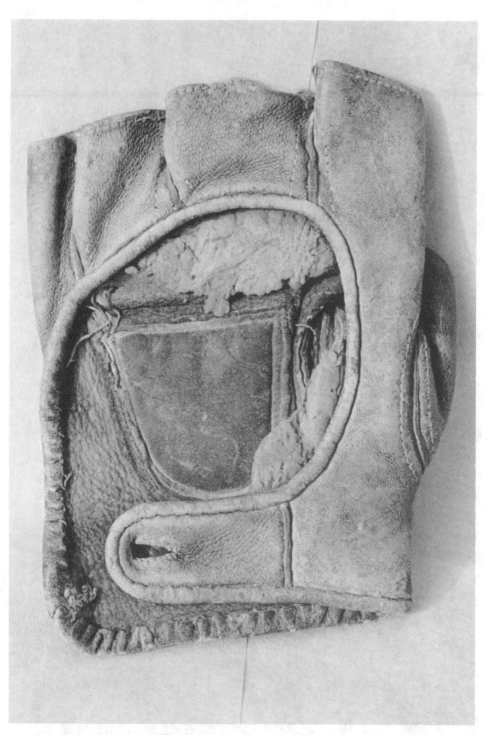

Close-up of back on 1880s fingerless glove. Notice padding on inside.

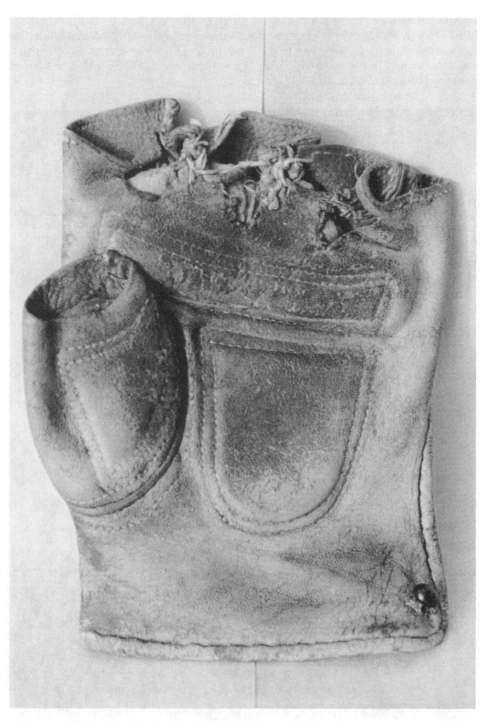

Close-up of face on 1880s fingerless glove. Notice the stitching on palm and thumb.

Ambidextrous gloves - An unusual glove in that it could be worn on either hand. The thumb and little finger are the same size and evenly spaced while the three fingers in between are straight. All of the fingers/thumbs have a thick solid web sewn between them much like the duck web. Dates from the turn of century through the World War I era.

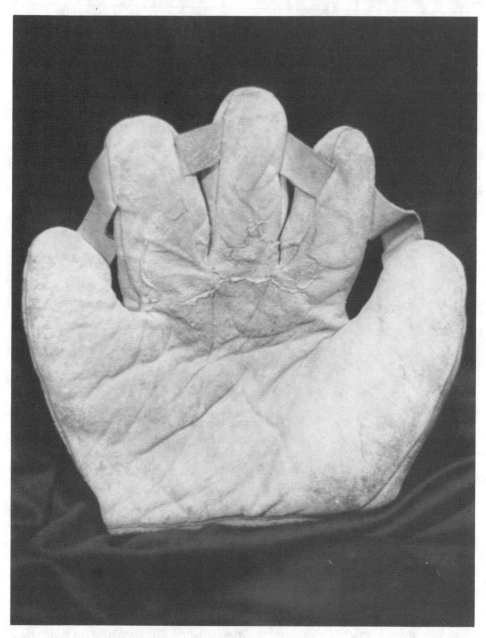

Thin web ambidextrous glove ca. 1900.

Reach ambidextrous glove ca. 1895-05.

Solid sewn web - Used on gloves approximately 1900-1910. A solid web sewn to thumb and first finger with only a hint of space at bottom. Web narrowed to about one inch from 1910-20 to allow more fielding flexibility but still sewn to thumb and finger.

Solid web - Unlike the sewn web, this style came into vogue during the 1940s. It is attached between thumb and first finger by means of a lacing system and metal eyelets.

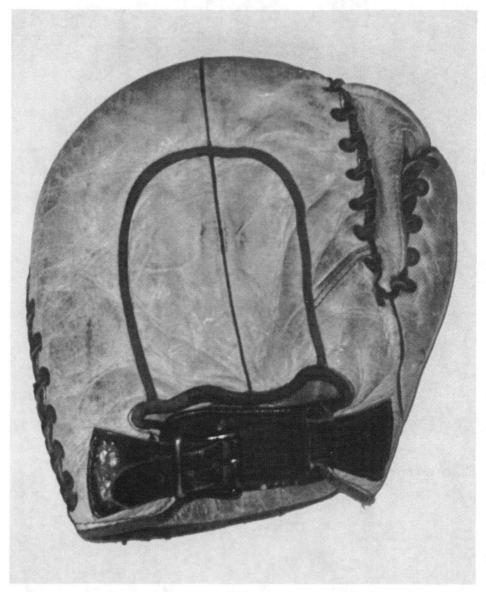

Back view of 1930s baseman's mitt with solid web.

Tunnel loop - A style of web, in series of one, two, three, or more one inch pieces of leather through which a leather lace passes and connects through metal eyelets as above. Circa 1930-40s. Gloves from the 1920s and early 1930s also used a single tunnel loop style web except that the loop is attached by means of rawhide laced through small tabs of leather sewn to the thumb and first finger. These are often found torn, thus the reason for the metal eyelets, which were more durable.

Buckle web - Used on early (circa 1910) basemans' and catchers' mitts. It was a buckle that joined the body of the mitt to the thumb thus acting like a web. To date, there has been no fielder's glove seen with this single buckle web.

Piping - The edging material used on gloves, sometimes leather, but also cloth, plastic coated cloth, and plastic.

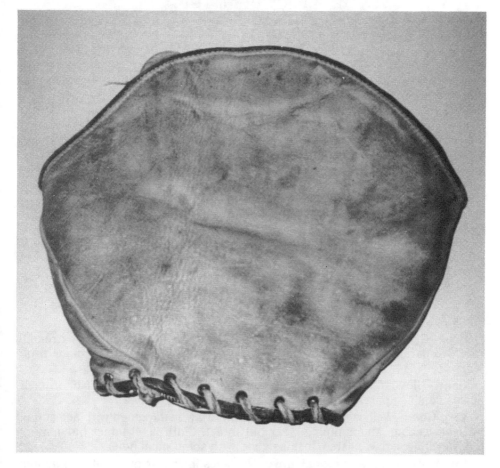

Face view of pocket glove showing no delineation of fingers, which are hidden in back.

Close-up of face on 1880s fingerless glove. Notice the stitching on palm and thumb.

Grading

Poor - Gloves in this condition are generally not collectible unless extremely rare. Irreparable tears, holes, dry rot, water damage, and other major problems.

Good - Glove that is well used, leather chaffed and thin in spots. No form left. Seams coming apart. Insides rotting and piping falling away.

Very Good - Well used but soft and supple. May be darkened with age and oil but serviceable. Minor piping wear but intact. Cloth label intact but may be indiscernible, if one existed. Insides good with some small holes.

Excellent - Nice, all original glove. No holes inside or out. Soft and supple, cloth patch intact and readable. Nice color and any imprinting on glove readable as well. Strong form.

Near Mint - Exactly that, almost new. All of its original color and form, all markings clear, patch perfect. Insides perfect

Mint - new or as new. New/old stock.

Price Guide

MIB (mint in box) - any boxed pre-1920 gloves are rare.

Pre-1900 at least 50% of listed mint price.

(1900-20) 40-50% of mint price.-

(1920-30) 30-40% of mint price.

(1930-45) 20-30% of mint price.

Postwar 10-20% of mint price.

Boxes with great illustrations or players pictured would be worth more.

Hang tags - as above, if illustrated with pictures, price individually. If plain with maker or model, add 10-20%.

For mint condition gloves, add 50% for pre-1920, 40% for 1920-45 period and 20% on postwar models. All prices listed for USA made gloves only.

Child models, those that an average man could not use in a game, deduct 30-50%. Many child model gloves used a lesser grade of material and craftsmanship.

Glove Type	V.G.	EXC.	NR/MT	SUPPLY
Fingerless (ea.)	$600	$1000	$1500	rare
Workman w/o web	$400	$800	$1200	rare
Workman w/web	$350	$750	$1000	rare
19th century baseman's mitts, small grommet or button back	$350	$750	$1000	rare
19th century catcher's	$250	$450	$650	varies
Duck web	$400	$800	$1200	rare
Ambidextrous glove	$500	$900	$1300	rare
Crescent pad	$250	$450	$650	common
Solid sewn full webs				
(1900-10)	$150	$300	$450	common
(1910-20) 1" web	$75	$125	$300	common

Catcher's mitts. Early catcher's and baseman's mitts have no cover on back of wrist, the leather belt extends across the expanse.

	V.G.	EXC.	NR/MT	SUPPLY
(1900-10)	$150	$300	$450	common
(1910-20)	$75	$125	$300	common
Baseman's mitts				
(1900-10)	$150	$300	$450	common
(1910-20)	$75	$125	$300	common

Miscellaneous prewar gloves (1920-45): catcher's, baseman's mitts, and fielders. Unless unusual such as zipper bottom or buckle webs, etc. These gloves survive in good numbers and are the least collectible of all prewar models.

	V.G.	EXC.	NR/MT	SUPPLY
	$50	$75	$125	common

Miscellaneous postwar gloves (1945-60): laced fingers, catcher's mitts with webs, trapper model first base mitts, etc. Again, not highly collectible unless like new. Popular for autographs.

	V.G.	EXC.	NR/MT	SUPPLY
	$20	$40	$60	common

Progression of Gloves from 1920-55

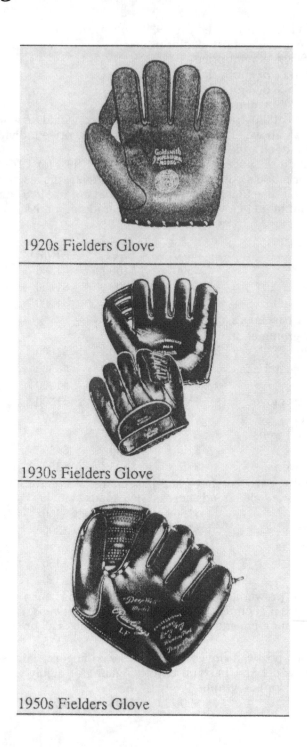

1920s Fielders Glove

1930s Fielders Glove

1950s Fielders Glove

Progression of Mitts from 1920-55

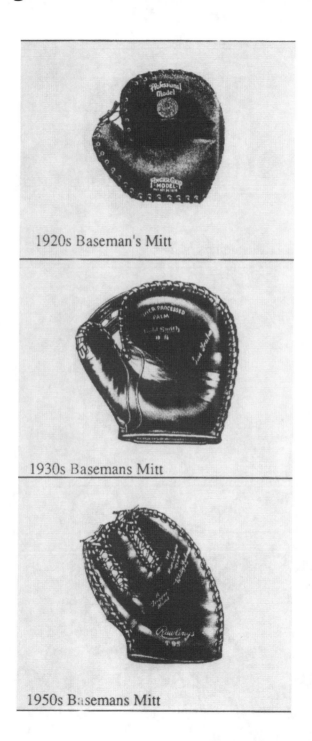

1920s Baseman's Mitt

1930s Basemans Mitt

1950s Basemans Mitt

Progression of Catchers Mitts from 1920-55

1920s Catchers Mitt

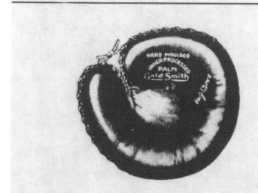

1930s Catchers Mitt

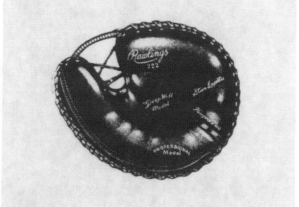

1950s Catchers Mitt

following diagrams of baseball glove webs provide a fairly accurate means of determining the approximate era that the ~e was produced. Sometimes the particular web shown covered two decades or more of production as glovemakers ~inued the design in their line because of its popularity and the economical use of existing production leather dies. The ~ods suggested cover the inception of early period of the web design.

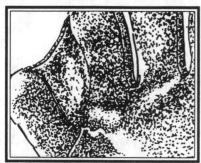

1900-1910: *The web is sewn directly into the thumb and forefinger and covers the bottom (crotch) to the top of the thumb forming a triangular pattern.*

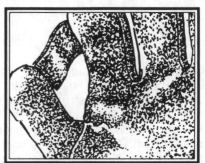

1910-1920: *To provide more flexibility between the thumb and forefinger the flat leather strip web was narrowed later on. This allowed the glove to more easily close around the ball than the tighter fastening triangular web used previously.*

1920-1925: *When Bill Doak designed his glove for Rawlings he provided for two rawhide laces to be sewn into the forefinger and thumb supplying even more flexibility that the flat piece leaher strip and soon the laces would become a constant part of the web, utilized in one form or another.*

1925-1930: *The two rawhide laces were being torn from the glove leather or breaking quite often so manufacturers tried lacing the webs together in various fashions but generally had settled on vertical tunnel pieces sewn to the forefinger and thumb then looped the rawhide laces through these openings.*

1930-1935: *The horizontal tunnel web was introduced and the rawhide laces run through these to form a better trap for the ball and to strengthen the overall web.*

1935-1940: *Two tunnel pieces then three were used on glove webs as the decade of the thirties ended. The full flat piece web wasn't introduced until the war time years.*

submitted by Joe Phillips

15

BATS

Bats, store models and gamers, show bats, autograph bats, block letter bats, foil imprint bats, black bats, brown bats, little league bats, post player bats, non-endorsed bats, mushroom bats, ring bats, decal bats, ball and handle bats, generic company bats, and on and on, well, you get the idea. So many bats, so little time. And the two questions on almost every mind: "Is it a gamer" or "What's it worth?" A store bat is one that any person could have bought at the local outfitter at a certain time (i.e. retail outlets) and a gamer is a bat supplied by a company for a major league player. There are also gamers supplied for colleges, semi-pros, and old-timer games. We cannot get into the specifics of all game model bats and this book deals only with the equipment available to the public. Most of the companies mentioned such as Reach, H&B (Hillerich & Bradsby), Adirondack, Spalding, Kren, Wright & Ditson and Hanna Batrite, made both professional game bats as well as store bats. To determine possible game use, one must look at dimensions, labeling periods, model numbers, wood, etc. and compare them with the player, his playing years and ordered models.

Glossary

Store bat - One that was available at a retail outlet.
Autograph series - Bears the likeness of a famous player's signature.
Foil bat - The signature is heat pressed with a black, lightly imprinted process rather than the deeply impressed models.

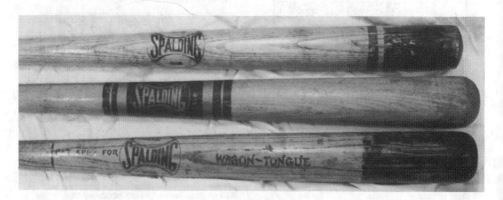

Three Spalding bats ca. 1880-1900.

Spalding Gold Medal decal bat ca. 1900.

Spalding Autograph bat, Phil Cavaretta, ca. 1940.

Little league bats - Generally marked as such or any bat shorter than 31 inches.

Block letter - Name of player is block style rather than script, i.e., Rogers Hornsby model or style.

Mushroom bat - Has large, egg-shaped knob, popular style from approximately 1900-1920.

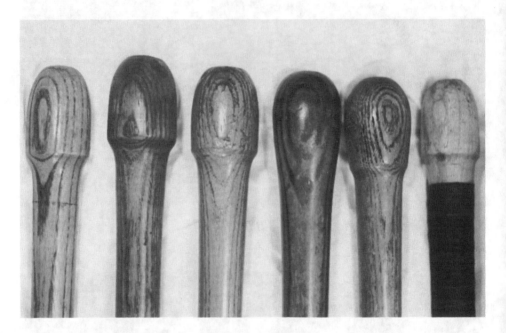

Variations on the mushroom knob ca. 1900-20.

Ring bat - Has painted rings around center and sometimes at the end of bat. A style popular before the turn of the century.

Decal bat - Has an applique somewhere on bat. (This style of bat has an entire chapter of its own.)

Generic bat - Has local markings such as Pontiac, Bee Hive, Campbell, etc. There are literally thousands of these private label bats.

Ball & handle bat - Has a large round wooden knob just a bit smaller than a baseball; popular during latter half of nineteenth century and early twentieth century.

Mini bat - Usually 18 inches or less, sold at stadiums and through mail.

Prewar model - Bat that bears the signature of players who played the majority of their careers before 1945. Bats of prewar players, i.e. Jimmie Foxx, made years after their actual playing days, will always bring less. The amount depends on how much later the bat was made.

Pre-1920 - As above, this applies to players who played the majority of their career before 1920.

Variations in knobs from mushrooms(l) to ball knob (center) to traditional. (right two).

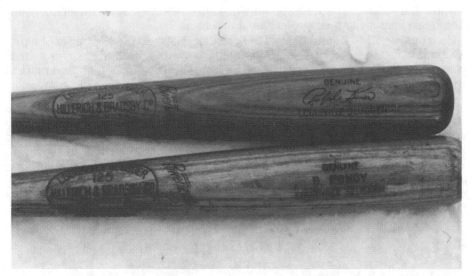

The top bat is a Ralph Kiner signature model. The bottom is a D. Fondy block letter model. Both are game-used H&B bats ca. 1949-59.

Postwar - Players who played the majority of their career after 1945. There will be players who split the above guidelines, but a happy medium should be obtainable.

Gamer - Bat made for use specifically for the major leagues and specially marked bats for minor league players.

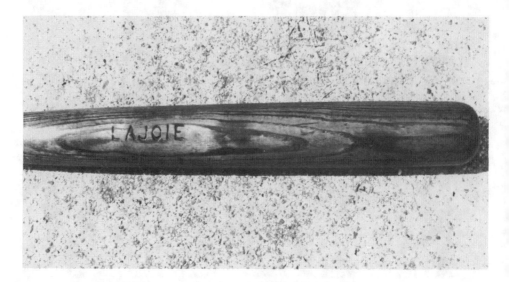

Early Nap Lajoie game bat, similar to Block style Wright & Ditson store bat except no maker's marks and hand rasped bat ends.

Show bat - Made for autograph shows, can sometimes be mistaken as game-used bats since many bear professional markings.

Coaches' or Old-Timers' bats - These usually have all the earmarks of a professional game bat except that the labeling period is after the player, whose name is inscribed on barrel, has retired. They will sometimes be found marked with special dates.

Black or brown World Series, All-Star, and Hall of Fame bats - The first two were never sold in stores and the Hall of Fame bats were issued by the Hall. All of these bats were made by H&B (Hillerich & Bradsby). The All-Star and World Series bats were manufactured during the years marked on bat and given to people related to the ball clubs. The Hall of Fame bats were retroactive to the first inductions. These bats were first offered through the Hall in the early 1980s. Since they were not available through the store trade, we will not cover the values in this book.

Grading

Fair/poor - Severely cracked with major pieces missing, name obliterated, dry rot, etc. Generally of value only as a decoration.

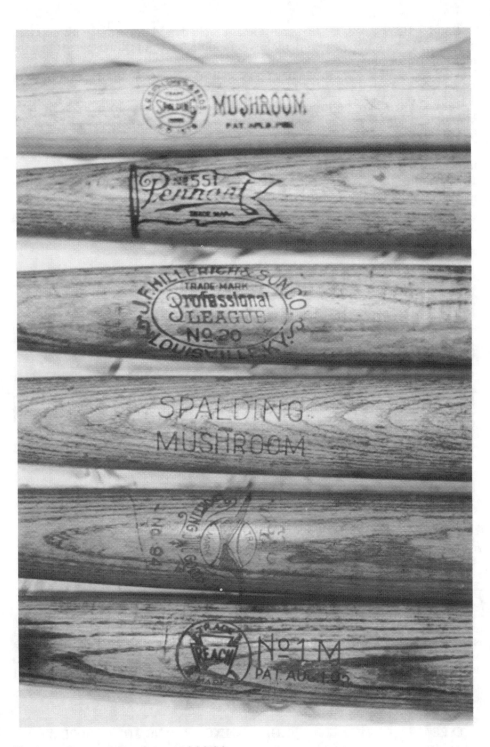

Various Center brands ca. 1900-20.

Good - Heavy use, grain separation, cracked and repaired with nails or screws, players name or company logo readable but light. Knob pieces may be missing. No original gloss or color. Major chipping with cleat or rock marks leaving small pieces of wood missing as well. May have small piece off back or handle.

Very Good - May be cracked but must be neat repair, no nails or screws, stamping readable but light, some minor grain separation but no pieces missing. Minor cleat marks. Some original gloss and color.

Excellent - No grain separation, medium use, no cracks or repairs, knob intact, stamping strong. Most original gloss and color. Minor cleat marks.

Near-Mint - Shows almost no use, no cracks, strong signature, no cleat marks, all original gloss, some minor ball marks and scuffs.

Mint - No use at all. Storage scuffs acceptable if minor and not covering markings.

Ty Cobb brand W.B. Jarvis Sporting Goods Company, Detroit and Grand Rapids, ca. 1915.

Price Guide

If mint, add 20% to prewar, 10% to postwar near-mint prices. If the bat has some qualities of a near-mint bat but other qualities closer to excellent, the value would be somewhere in between. If an item is marked little league, regardless of player or length, it has little or no value. To date, anything marked softball suffers a similar fate and would probably only be desired by decorators.

TYPE	V.G.	EXC.	NR/MT	SUPPLY
Mushroom bat	$125	$200	$350	common

THE SPALDING MUSHROOM BAT

PATENTED

IN this bat a principle has been utilized which makes a bat of the same weight many times more effective than the ordinary style under certain conditions, and as an all-round bat we have received many letters from prominent professional players testifying to their appreciation of the good points of its construction. They say: "Both balance and model are perfect." And in quality of timber the grade is the same as that used in our best Autograph bats. The knob arrangement at the end of the bat enables us to get a more even distribution of weight over the whole length than is possible under the old construction, and for certain kinds of play the bat is practically invaluable.

We recommend it heartily to our customers, feeling certain that they will find in the combination of good qualities which it possesses something that they have sought for in vain elsewhere — a perfect bat.

THE SPALDING MUSHROOM BAT, $1.00

NEW YORK, Sept. 22, 1903.
For a long time I have been trying to find a bat that would balance when choking. Not until I used the Mushroom Bat, invented by Jack Pickett, have I found a bat that was up to my idea. This bat is used exclusively by the New York players. Yours truly, JOHN J. McGRAW,
Manager New York B. B. Club.

In all my experience as a base ball player I have not found a more satisfactory base ball bat than the Spalding Mushroom Bat. The timber is the best I have seen; he balance and model of the bat is perfect. Yours truly,
JAMES J. CALLAHAN,
Manager-Captain Chicago American League Club.

CHICAGO, Oct. 14, 1903.
I have played professional base ball for the last fifteen years, and have tried all kinds of bats, but no bat has given me such good service as the Spalding Mushroom bat, introduced by Jack Pickett. Quality and balance are perfect. Yours truly, WM. GLEASON,
Captain Philadelphia National League B. B. Club.

CHICAGO, Oct. 14, 1903.
The Spalding Mushroom Bat, introduced by Jack Pickett, receives my hearty endorsement. My experience as a ball player enables me to thoroughly appreciate its good qualities. Yours truly,
CHAS. A. COMISKEY,
President Chicago American League Club.

CHICAGO, Oct. 14, 1903.
In all our experience as base ball players we have not found a bat more satisfactory than the Spalding Mushroom Bat, introduced by Jack Pickett.

JAMES F. SLAGLE	JOHN EVERS	F. L. CHANCE
J. KLING	J. McCARTHY	JOE TINKER
DR. J. P. CASEY	D. JONES	Of Chicago Nat. League Club

7

Mushroom bats for sale in the 1904 Spalding Spring/Summer Sports Catalog.

Ring bat; must be at least 36", makers' name visible, ca. 1880s and 1890s. Usual length is about 40". For shorter bats or bats with stripes but no makers name, deduct 50%.

Spalding with logo	$350	$600	$1000	rare
Other makers	$250	$500	$900	rare
Ball & handle bats	$250	$500	$900	rare

Generic bats 1900-1945, unless unusual, i.e. bottle bat, stunning logo, etc, these are the most common & least collected bats. Watch for interesting logos. An interesting collection could be amassed for a small sum.

$35	$50	$95	common

Postwar player model signature bats must be at least 34". Undersize bats are basically not collectible. There will be slight premiums for college bats as these are professional model bats but bear college markings, usually under the player's name, such as USC or LFC. The amount of premium depends on the player, Hall of Famers ("Hofers") 20%, stars 10%, Mantle or DiMaggio add additional 20% both for college bats and store models. The following postwar prices are for all makers, Adirondack, H&B, Hanna Batrite, and any of the sundry other companies applying player's names to their line of bats.

Hall of Fame Members

Signature engraved	$25	$45	$65	common
Signature foil	$15	$25	$45	common
Block name	$15	$25	$45	common

Star & Common Players

Signature engraved	$20	$40	$60	common
Signature foil	$15	$25	$45	common
Block name	$10	$20	$30	common

Prewar bats - includes Spalding, Reach, Kren, Batrite, and others except H&B prewars.
Hall of fame - pre 1920 (1920-45 deduct 20-30%).

Signature	$250	$400	$600	varies
Block	$200	$350	$500	varies
Exceptions:				
Wright & Ditson				
Lajoie double knob, block	$600	$1000	$1800	rare
Same w/single knob,	$500	$800	$1200	rare
Gehrig Batrite(bat logo)	$400	$600	$800	common
Cobb(Spalding 1908)	$400	$600	$800	rare
Ray Schalk(Spalding 1924)	$400	$600	$800	rare

Early 1890s Spalding Wagon-Tongue bat.

Center label of early J.F. Hillerich & Son without Bradsby, 1916.

Adirondack Cobb, Gehrig, & Ruth bats, not made until after mid 1940s	$75	$125	$200	common

Stars - pre 1920 as above (1920-45 deduct 20-30%).

Signature	$100	$150	$250	varies
Block	$75	$125	$200	varies
Exceptions:				
Hal Chase (Spalding 1919-20)	$300	$500	$700	rare
Heinie Zimmerman (Spalding)	$200	$350	$500	rare

Hillerich & Bradsby Bats

All prices listed are for vintage, deeply etched bats, Model 125s of at least 34" (bats 32-33" deduct 20%). Bats shorter than 32" will be worth half or less (Models 40, 50, 250 and other signature models, deduct 10%). (Foil bats deduct 20-50% depending on condition of foil print.) Block model bats such as Models #14, #9, #8, etc., listed under block letter prices.

YMCA marked bats manufactured for servicemen during World War I 1917-19 are professional model bats. Add 20-50%.

Prewar Hall of Famers, known endorsed models

PLAYER	V.G.	EXC.	NR/MT	SUPPLY
Gehrig	$200	$350	$500	common
Ruth	$200	$350	$500	common
Cobb	$200	$350	$500	common
DiMaggio	$150	$300	$400	rare
E. Collins	$100	$200	$300	common
F. Baker	$100	$200	$300	common
Greenberg	$100	$200	$300	common
Lazzari	$100	$200	$300	rare
E. Lombardi	$100	$200	$300	rare
Speaker	$150	$300	$400	common
H. Wagner	$150	$300	$400	rare
Others	$75	$135	$200	varies
Block letters	$50-75	$75-100	$1-125	varies

Prewar stars - known models

Joe Jackson	$500	$800	$1200	rare
Others	$50	$100	$150	varies
Block	$25-50	$50-75	$75-100	varies

There are no known H&B store bats of any other Black Sox stars, i.e., Buck Weaver, Hap Felsch, Chick Gandil, Swede Risberg, Fred McMullin, Eddie Cicotte, or Lefty Williams. These bats, if turned up, either in block letters or script, would have a value of about 60% of listed Jackson prices. Beware of made-up bats with block letter last names. As prices increase, so do forgeries. Since there is no evidence of any of the above store bats ever being made, the chances of finding one, unless some period prototype, is impossible. Bats of these players may have been made by sundry other small companies, but be careful.

Mini Bats

TYPE	V.G.	EXC.	NR/MT	SUPPLY
Prewar Hofers	$45	$65	$85	varies

Ruth, Wagner, Cobb, Cy Young, Gehrig and DiMaggio add 10-20%

TYPE	V.G.	EXC.	NR/MT	SUPPLY
Prewar stars	$30	$50	$65	varies
Postwar Hofers	$10	$20	$30	varies
Postwar stars	$5	$10	$20	varies

World Series Souvenir Bats

Pre-1920 - $200 and up. Almost impossible to find.
1921-45 - $100 and up. Certain years are really tough.
1946-59 - $75. Almost every year is highly sought, all Dodgers,
        Yankees, 1946 Red Sox, 1959 White Sox, and 1957 Braves.
1960-71 - 1960, 1961, 1965, and 1971, $50-75.
Others usually $50 or less.

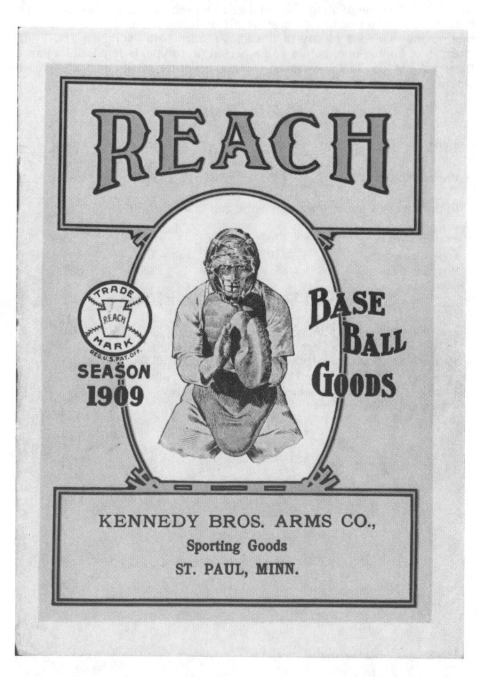

Front cover of the A.J. Reach Company 1909 Season Catalog, Philadelphia.

Back cover of the A.J. Reach Company 1909 Season Catalog, Philadelphia.

LOUISVILLE SLUGGERS

No. 40K. Made of choicest selected second growth Ash with our new Cork Grip handle. The cork absorbs the perspiration and prevents vibration. Made in different models. Lengths 32 to 36 inches. Oil tempered finish, one in a paper bag . . . . Each **$1.50**
No. 45K. Same style as 40K., only Boys size . . . . Each **1.00**

No. 125. Made from choicest selected second growth Ash, straight grain, hand turned oil tempere finish, which gives the wood a hard surface and good driving power. Lengths 32 to 36 inches. . Each **$1.0**

No. 40TC. TY COBB Bat, made from second growth Ash, straight grain, hand turned. Made from model used by the famous slugger. Flame burnt finish, highly polished. Lengths 32 to 36 inches.
Each   **$1.00**
No. 40TCJ. TY COBB, Jr., is the same as 40TC., only Junior size, 32 in. Long . . Each **.50**

No. 40FB. "Good Night" FRANK BAKER Model. Exact duplicate of the bat used by Baker in world's series. Made from selected second growth Ash, golden mottled finish. Lengths 33, 34 and 35 inches
Each   **$1.00**
No. 40W. HANS WAGNER Model is made from choicest timber, hand turned with golden finish. Wagner trade mark. Lengths 32 to 36 inches . . . . Each **$1.00**
No. 40WJ. HANS WAGNER Junior Model, same as 40W., only 32 inches long . "   **.50**

No. 40EC. Made from choicest stock, modeled for Eddie Collins, the famous player of Philadelphia Athletics. Golden mottled finish. Lengths 33, 34 and 35 inches . . . . Each **$1.00**
No. 40HD. HARRY DAVIS Model. Second growth Ash, hand turned, thin handle with hitting surface well toward the end. Lengths 32 to 36 inches . . . . Each **$1.00**

No. 40TS. TRIS SPEAKER Model. Used by the famous player in the world's series. Selected timber, hand turned, perfectly balanced. Lengths 32 to 36 inches . . . . Each **$1.00**

No. 40JJ. JOE JACKSON Model. Hand turned, selected second growth Ash, special burnished dark finish, medium size handle, nicely balanced. Lengths 33 to 36 inches . . . . Each **$1.00**
No. 40T. Made from choice second growth stock, hand turned designed from leading player's model; natural finish, highly polished. Taped Handle. Lengths 32 to 35 inches . . . . Each **$0.85**

ALSO THE FOLLOWING MODELS

No. 40 L   Napoleon Lajoie . . . . Each   1.00
No. 40 HG   Hank Gowdy . . . . Each   1.00
No. 40LJ   Same as 40L, only boy's size . . . . Each   .50
No. 40ECJ   Same as 40EC, only boy's size . . . . Each   .50

A page from the 1917 Schoverling, Daly & Gales catalog featuring the various decal bats being offered by Hillerich & Bradsby. (Bradsby's name appeared on H & B bats in 1916. Since this 1917 catalog shows bats without his name, this is an indication that the catalog used old drawings.)

DECAL BATS

Decal bats may be the most aesthetically beautiful pieces of equipment ever manufactured. Decals appear both in large and small sizes, with images of noted players or generic forms, with vibrant colors and model names. They appear on the barrels as well as center labels. These bats were made by Hillerich & Bradsby, Stahl & Dean, Spalding, A.J. Reach, and sundry smaller firms, and like baseball cards and other collectibles, condition is everything.

A decal bat is a bat on which an appliqué has been affixed. Hillerich & Bradsby came out with their player series of decal bats in 1905 after signing Pirates slugging star, Honus Wagner, as a Louisville endorsee. These bats, with their beautiful color pictures on the barrels, resemble the T206 cards applied to a bat. They were offered on several full-size player bats, as well as on the smaller souvenir bats. The list of known player model prewar decal bats is as follows; Honus Wagner, Tris Speaker, Eddie Collins, George Sisler, Nap Lajoie, Hank Gowdy, Jake Daubert, Ty Cobb, Frank Baker, Joe Jackson, and Harry Davis, all stars from the 1920s or earlier. Several of these bats come in different variations. The Jackson, although only seen with the image of him with his Cleveland hat, comes in two background color variations. The same holds true for the Wagner. The Davis, Gowdy, Baker, Sisler, and Collins bats have only been seen in one style. Lajoie comes in both a full-body batting pose and a profile model. Speaker was available with two completely different profile shots, and Cobb is known to exist in at least four different poses. There are possibly others but this is what is known to exist to date.

In addition to these early decal bats, H&B revived the decal player model bats in the mid 1950s with a series of bats that included Babe Ruth, Mickey Mantle, Ferris Fain, Jackie Robinson, Ted Williams, Ralph Kiner, and Joe DiMaggio. The Mantle and Fain have turned up in lengths of 34 inches while the others have all been little league bats, at least to date. Each has a head portrait of the player set against a contrasting background.

H&B also produced many bats with no player pictures at all. A mid-1920s catalog listed a series of decal bats with the American Shield and a facsimile player's signature underneath, but with no photograph. They were offered with autograph transfers of Ruth, Cobb, Roush, Lajoie, Baker, Collins, Wagner, Sisler, Daubert, Speaker, Gowdy, and Jackson. I'm sure there were other models offered in different years, but without a catalog or an example, the list would be hard to complete. Other bats have words like Professional, League, etc. on the barrel set against vibrant background color.

Stahl & Dean manufactured picture decal bats, known as the "American Biffer" series, as well as examples with model names on the barrel. The Biffer series features a picture of the player with a facsimile autograph beneath and

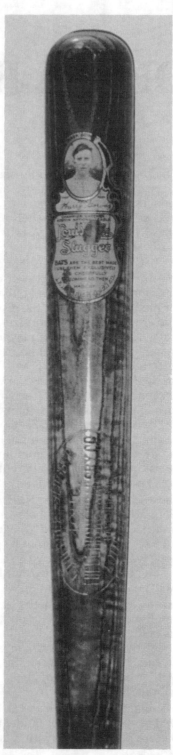

Left: Close-up of Ty Cobb decal bat showing 1911-15 center label.
Right: Close-up of Hank Gowdy brown decal bat with 1921 center label.

the facsimile autograph burned into the center of the bat. Player models include Tris Speaker, Ping Bodie, and Jim Delahanty. There are probably others but early Stahl & Dean catalogs are as scarce as the bats.

The A.J. Reach Company made their top-of-the-line Burley model, which features a player with a bat on his shoulder and wearing a turned up collar, but there is no team or player affiliation aside from a resemblance to Cubs infielder Johnny Evers. Other Reach decal bats feature the round logo on the barrel. To date, there have been no Famous Player picture models found, either in catalogs or examples.

Spalding used small Gold Medal decals on some of their early bats as well as stenciled stripes and logos. It was in the mid-1930s that they introduced their player model Resilite series with a beautiful black, gold, and silver center logo decal with the facsimile autograph on the barrel of players such as Gabby Hartnett, Heinie Manush, Hack Wilson, and a host of others.

Another of the more popular and valuable decal bats was the Black Betsy model. Offered in the late teens and early twenties, the bat featured a circular decal with the Spalding logo and the Black Betsy name set against the Black bat made famous by Joe Jackson. It is quite stunning.

There were probably other companies who issued a model bat with some form of decal but these are the examples most frequently encountered. If you do come across one, how do you grade it or put some sort of value on this piece? That's a tough question insomuch as you can have a decal that is 90 percent complete, but the missing 10 percent might be the name and head, thus the value is lost. Another 90 percent complete bat may contain the entire picture, with only peripheral chipping, and its value would be substantial.

So what are the guidelines? Grade a decal bat on the amount of decal remaining and make sure that the same holds true for the picture and autograph section. A 90 percent decal bat would have the full percentage of decal throughout,

Generic decal H&B bat with great graphics of ballplayers.

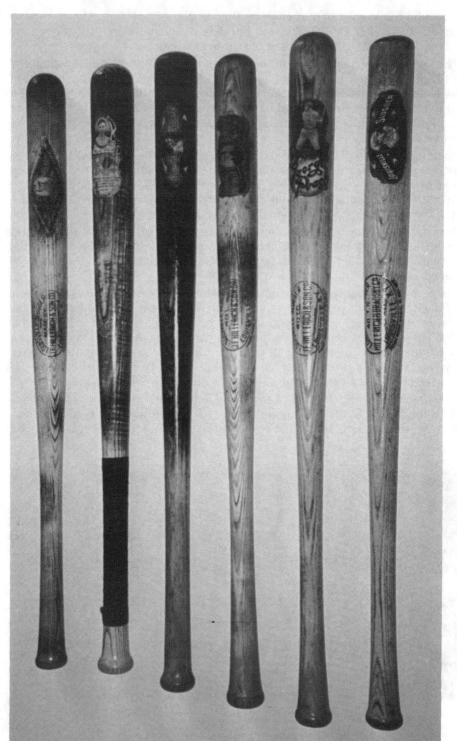

Collection of decal bats ca. 1905-20.

with the important features, the image and autograph, having only minor chipping.

Although image and autographs do not apply to decal bats bearing only the logos, they will be graded in the same method in regards to percentage of remaining decal. The condition of the bat is also important but secondary to the decal. I generally find that if the decal is really nice, the bat is generally in like condition.

So what are the decal bats worth on today's market? Like cards, each must be evaluated separately based on condition of the decal first, the bat next. Values for full-size bats are always greater than their small souvenir counterparts or bats shorter than 32 inches, the shortest length offered as a full-size decal bat. Decal bats picturing Hall of Fame players are worth a premium over their non-Hall of Fame competition, but not as much as one might think, since the decal bats of these players are sometimes scarcer than the Hall of Famers. This means collectors trying to collect all of the available player model decal bats in top condition might have a harder time adding a Jake Daubert to their collection, than say a Ty Cobb model.

As to the restoration of some decal bats, it is a personal matter for the buyer and will affect value depending on the work performed and the quality of the work. The price could go in either direction and would have to be handled on an individual basis. Decal bats that have over 70 percent of their original image with a good name and picture should be left alone–at least that is the consensus of most decal bat collectors. Decal bats are one item that should always be viewed in person before deciding on values. If you buy one through the mail based on a photograph, make sure you have return privileges.

Price Guide

Deduct 20-30% if bat is cracked or somewhat rough.

Some decals will fade or lose the outer image. This will decrease value by at least one grade. As for rarity, all nice decal bats should be considered rare.

PLAYER	% 100	90	80	70	60	50 OR LESS
Jackson	$4000	$3000	$2000	$1500	$1200	$800 down

(Lajoie and Wagner would be in the same range as Jackson.)

Cobb	$3500	$2500	$1800	$1300	$1100	$700 down

Collins, Baker, Speaker, Sisler, and other Hofers

	$2500	$1800	$1600	$1300	$1100	$700 down

Stars - This would include any other player model bats featuring images of the player such as Gowdy, Davis, Daubert, or Ping Bodie et al.

	$2000	$1600	$1300	$1000	$700	$500 down

Small size decal bats, 16-18", usually sell at about half the price of their larger counterparts.

Signature decal bats with no pictures of the player.

Beautiful decal bats of Frank Baker, Nap Lajoie, and Tris Speaker ca. 1905-20.

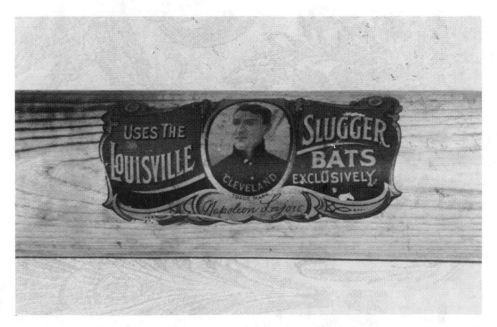

Close-up of Nap Lajoie decal bat in near mint 95% condition.

Condition	%100	90	80	70	60	50 or less
Hofers	$600	$500	$400	$350	$300	$200 down
Stars	$500	$400	$350	$300	$250	$150 down
Reach Burley	$600	$500	$400	$350	$300	$200 down
Spalding Black Betsy	$2000	$1500	$1000	$800	$600	$500

(Any clean Black Betsy model, regardless of decal, would be in the 50% range providing the bat and markings are nice.)

H&B mid-1950s decal bat series. List prices for full size.(Bats shorter than 33", deduct 10-30%)

Hofers	$400	$350	$300	$200	$150	$100 down
Stars	$300	$250	$200	$150	$100	$50 down

Bats with decals on barrel with models i.e. professional, league, etc.

	$300	$250	$200	$150	$100	$50 down

Spalding Resilite bats with player's name on barrel and center decal. Use percentage for center label. Player's name must be readable.

Hofers	$400	$350	$300	$200	$150	$100 down
Stars	$350	$300	$250	$175	$125	$75 down

Close-up of Tris Speaker decal bat in near mint 95% condition.

Close-up of Frank Baker decal bat in near mint 90% condition.

Ty Cobb and Hank Gowdy decal bats.

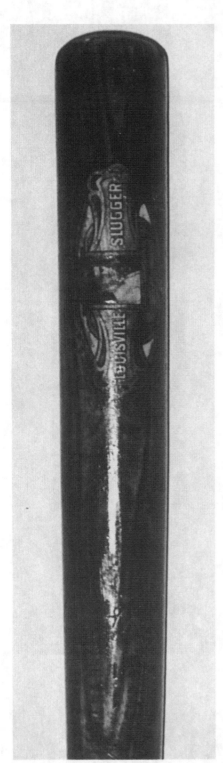

Shoeless Joe Jackson decal bat.

CATCHER'S MASKS

Ever since Harvard player Fred Thayer invented the catcher's mask for then Harvard catcher James Tyng, players facing 100 mile per hour fastballs scrambled to their local blacksmith, and then to A.G. Spalding, for the new fangled face cages. As with anything ever invented, from the moment of inception, there was a multitude of others wanting to improve it.

Catchers' masks included throat protectors, hinged ear protectors, built-in sun visors, and straps that would attach to the chest protector so that when the catcher threw off his mask to chase a ball, it might hang handily from his back rather than lie despondent in the dust.

Spiderman masks, spitters, bird cage style, and sundry other terms are now bandied about by vintage equipment collectors looking to add another cage to

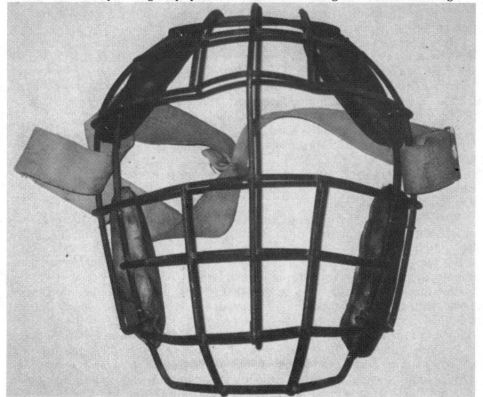

A semi-spider mask with early wired small pads ca. 1910.

their collection. With hundreds of individual patterns and styles, it can become a ceaseless endeavor, never knowing when another never-before-seen style may appear. They are almost three-dimensional primitive art forms, bent steel, horsehair and leather, all blended together to form the grotesque, Middle Ages' apparatus reminiscent of an Arthurian torture device now known as the catcher's mask. And collected they are, so making some sort of sense concerning the terms and styles of these aberrations may be in order. Herein lies the basics needed to identify and categorize, as best as one can, given the insurmountable varieties that now exist and those yet to be uncovered.

Glossary

Spider mask - This is a term used by collectors to describe the style of mask popular between 1890-1920. The eyes appear to be wide open circles resembling glasses (or the mask worn by comic book hero Spiderman) and narrowing at the bridge of the nose.

Bird cage - As above, same time frame, intricate wire pattern, but most, but not all, still exhibit the spider style eye design. Also may have forehead straps, small pads wired to cage, flat chin piece, and all other early characteristics of an early mask but without the Spiderman style of eye opening.

Padding - This is the covering surrounding the inside of the mask to cushion the blow of the ball to the face. It may be made of leather, canvas, a combination of both, or vinyl (late models).

Throat protector - An extension of the mask, usually with some leather padding, to protect the catcher's or umpire's throat. It is attached to the bottom of the mask and extends downward towards the chest.

Wire - The term used to describe the metal in the mask. The thickness of the wire, or cage, often determines the intended use i.e., sandlot ball with 20 mile per hour pitches, or the big leagues and high velocity.

Straps or headgear - This is what holds the mask to the face and on the head. Usually made of leather or canvas. It is attached to the mask with buckles.

Ear protectors - A protruding section of wire from side of mask to protect ear. Umpire masks were made with ear protectors that were hinged to allow them to move forward and back.

Visor - A piece of leather, cardboard, or tinted plastic attached to inside top of mask to block sun from the catcher's eyes. Popular from the late 1890s through the 1930s.

Spitters - This is a style of mask that has an opening for spitting tobacco. Popular style from the teens through the thirties.

Cast masks (also known as bar masks) - These are the composition metal masks with the solid bars. Although they are thought to be of recent vintage, solid bar composition metal masks date back to the early 1920s. If the pads are snapped to the metal, they are considered to be of the postwar variety or style.

Endorsed masks - These are masks that bear the facsimile signature of a famous catcher (or player whose name would sell anything). These names appear imprinted on the head strap or the chin pads. Some known models include Mickey Mantle, Yogi Berra, Stan Lopata, Bill Dickey, Bubbles Hargrave, Mickey Cochrane, Ray Schalk, Sherm Lollar, and Mort Cooper.

Early spider mask ca. 1910 with leather sun visor and hooked cage.

Early large bead spider mask ca. 1910.

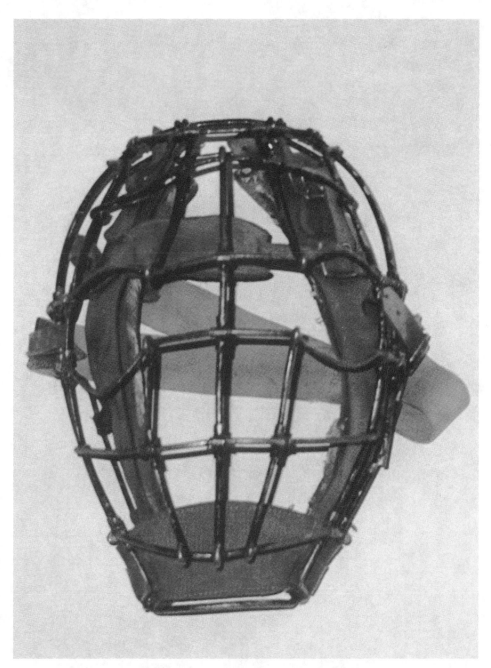

Spider mask with hooked cage, small pads, and forehead strap ca. 1890-1910.

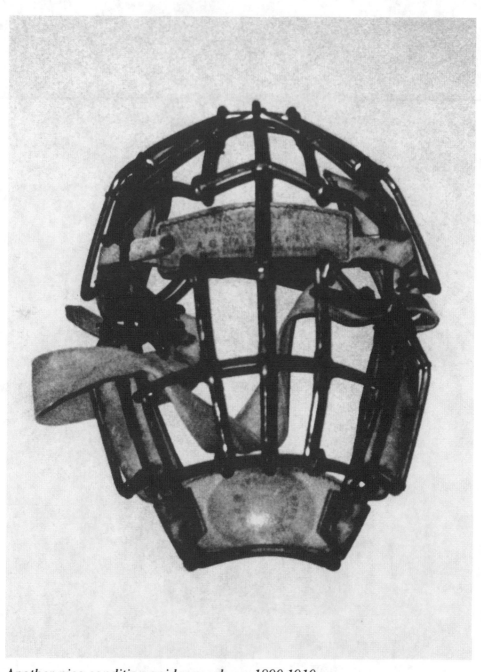

Another nice condition spider mask ca. 1890-1910.

Spider mask with all early features ca. 1900.

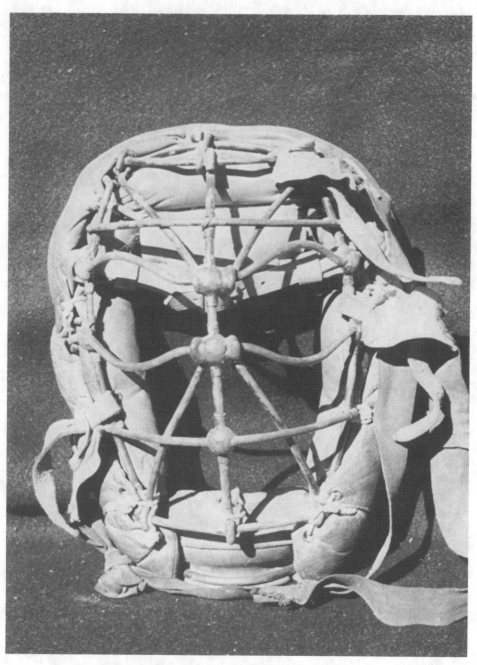

Spider mask with rare large bead joints ca. 1910-20.

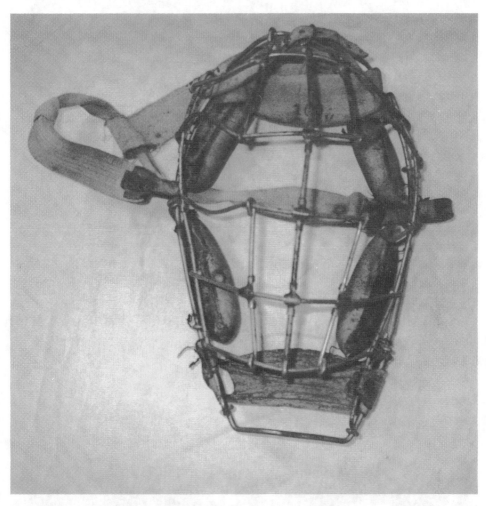

Early elongated spider mask with forehead and chin straps, (+) joints, and small pads ca. 1890-1910.

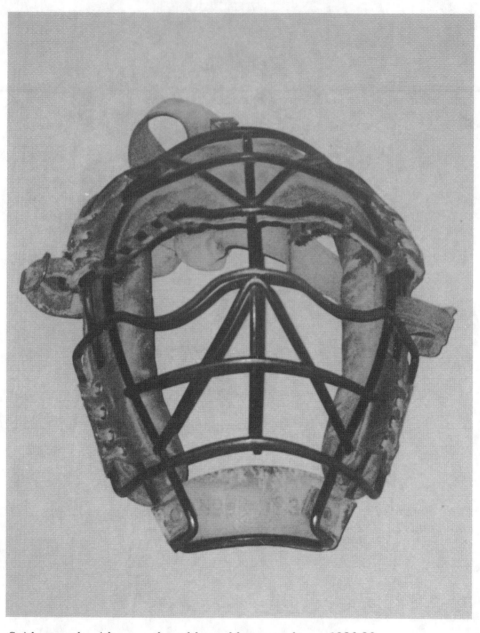

Spider mask with smooth welds and large pads ca. 1920-30.

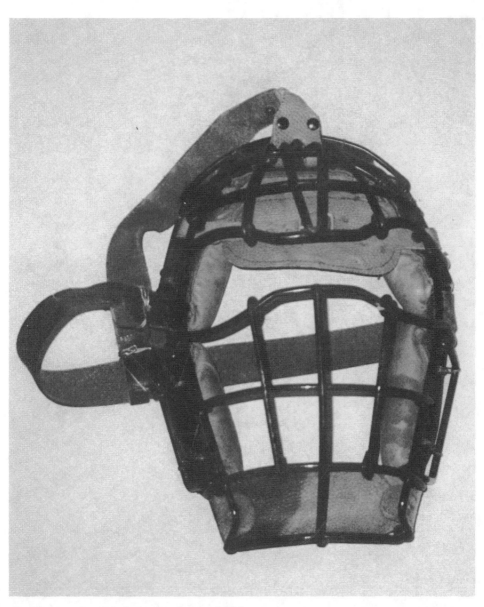

Spider mask with large pads ca. 1920s.

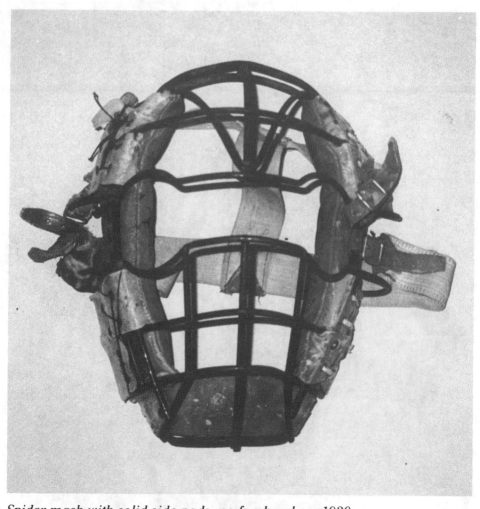

Spider mask with solid side pads, no forehead ca. 1920s.

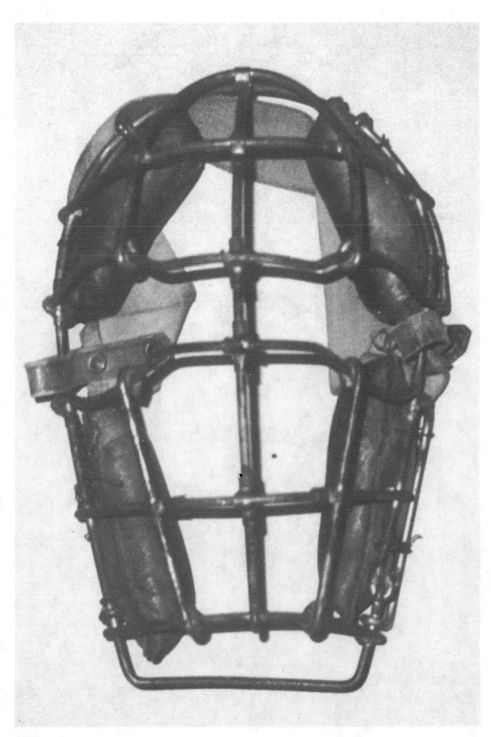

Elongated spider mask with small side pads ca 1890-1910.

Spider mask with oblong spitter ca. 1920s.

Thin wire spider mask ca. 1920s.

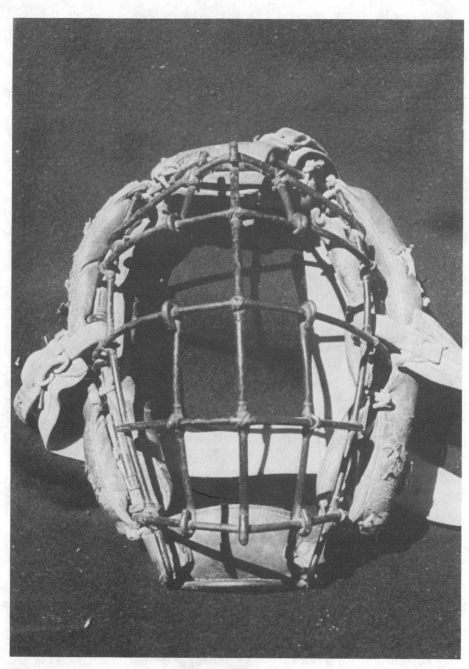

Birdcage mask ca. 1920s.

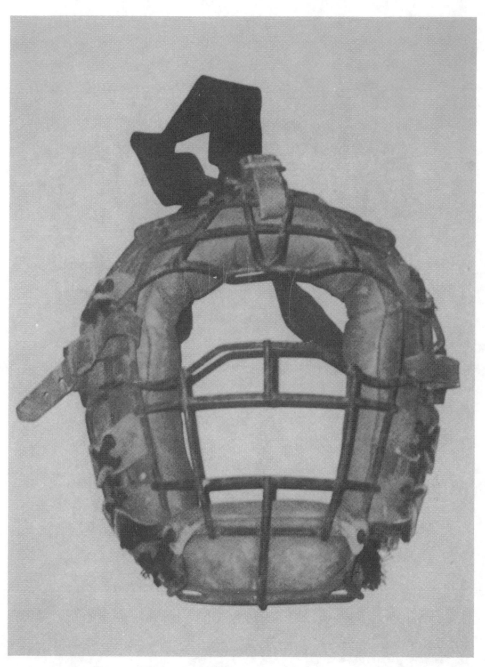

Wide spider mask with solid padding ca. 1920s.

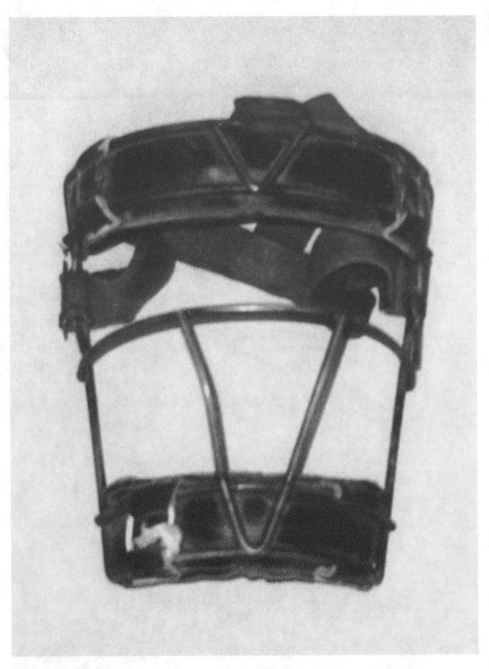

Typical softball mask ca. 1940-50 with pads at top and bottom only, extremely large spaces.

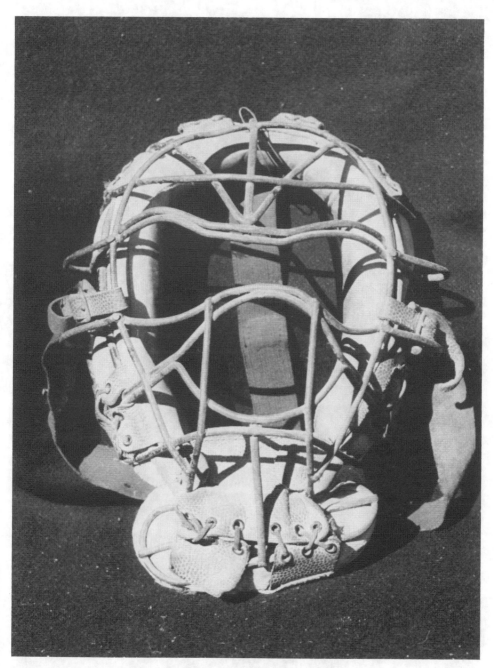

Spider mask with throat protector ca. 1920s.

Rare large bead spider mask with throat protector ca. 1900-20.

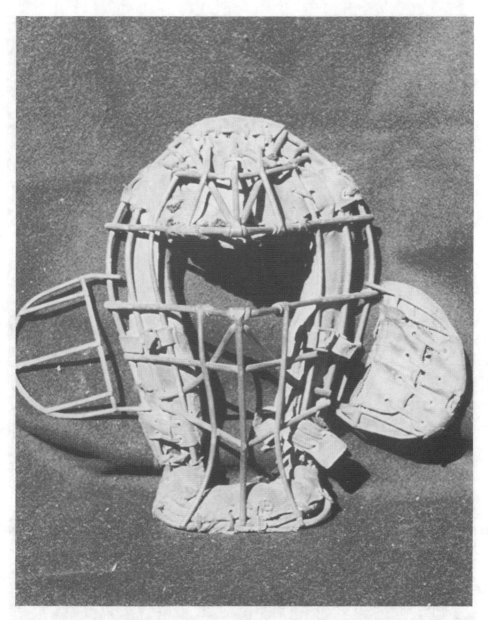

Early umpire's style mask with hinged ears, throat protector, and pointed face ca. 1900-20.

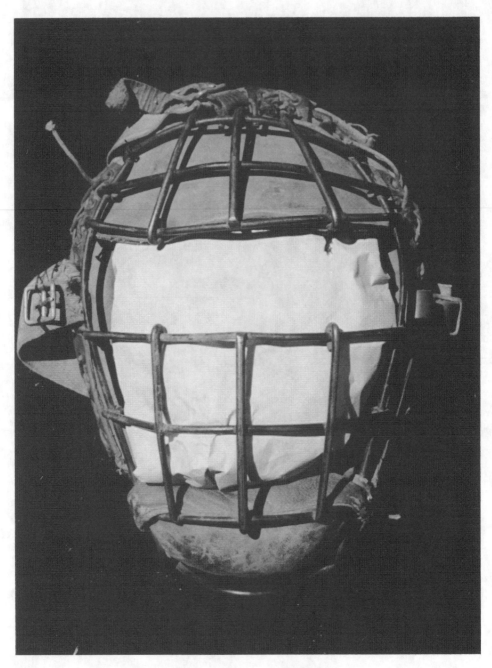

Horizontal bar mask with leather visor ca. 1920-30.

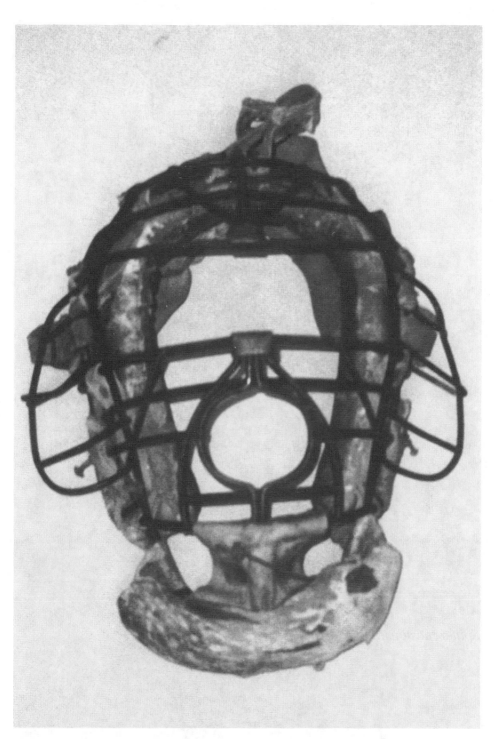

Spitter mask with rare throat protector ca. 1920s.

Spitter mask with odd keyhole version spitter ca. 1940s.

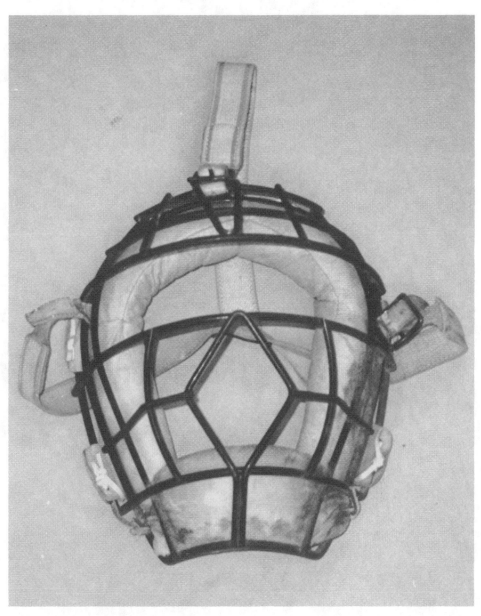

Diamond spitter mask ca. 1930-40.

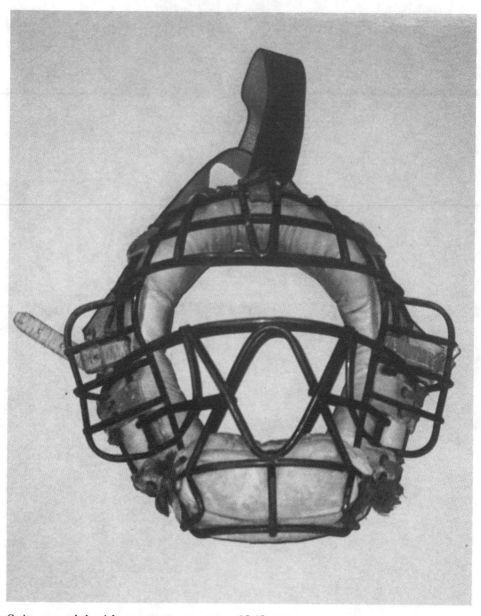

Spitter model with ear protectors ca. 1940s.

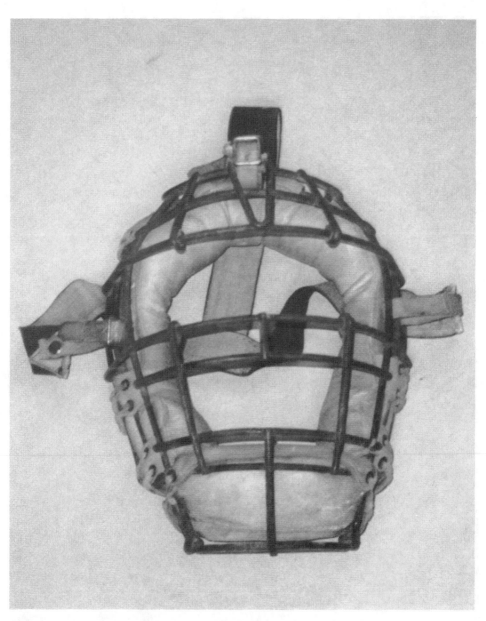

Typical horizontal bar mask ca. 1940.

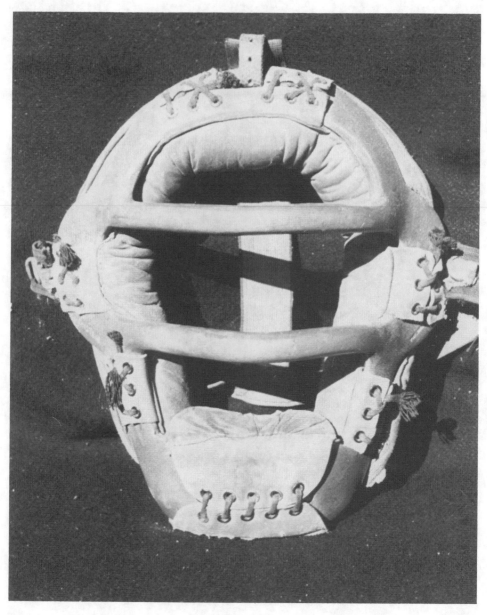

Molded bar mask ca. 1920-40. Notice that pads are strapped in and not snapped.

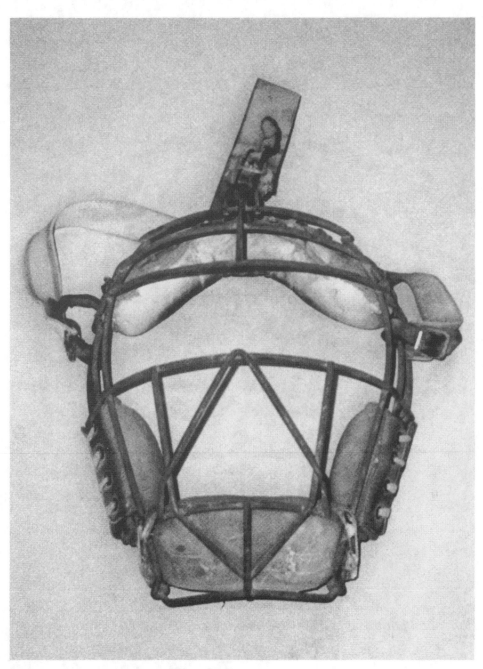

Horizontal bar mask ca. 1940-50.

Horizontal bar mask in like new condition ca. 1940s.

Notes On Masks

Early masks usually will be found with short leather pads, about three inches in length, wired to the cage with brass. In addition, early masks tend to come to a point in front, almost like a fencing mask. At the junctions where the horizontal bars meet the vertical ones, they are connected by means of bead welds (extremely scarce), hooked ends in which they are bent around each other like a hanger, and small + shaped pieces of metal that lie over the tops of the adjoining pieces where they cross. Early masks are also found with flat adjustable pieces of leather stretched across the inside of the mask for the forehead. In addition, the chin piece is also a flat piece of leather. Spider masks with the full pads around the inside of the face and laced to the cage with rawhide date from the 1920s.

Masks that have the pads snapped to the cage rather than laced date from the post-World War II era. Masks that only have the pads on the top of the face and at the bottom are softball masks. Neither of these style of masks are highly collected and hence have little value.

Early flat-steel masks–resembling a fencing mask except that the bars are flat with rivets holding them together–are probably the scarcest of all masks. Called the Howland Mask of 1878, one resides in the Hall of Fame and none are known to exist in any private collection. Needless to say, if one did turn up, it would be the prize of any collection.

Next in line would be the early, full-size versions of the Fred Thayer mask of 1875. A rather odd-looking mask in that it is long, similar in shape to half a football. Lined with canvas pads, the mask comes to a point in front and the horizontal wires wrap around a center vertical wire that runs the distance of the mask. Again, this model resides in the hall of fame and I know of only one example in a private collection.

The early full-size bird cage and spider masks are next in line and are the earliest form of mask most collectors may ever hope to own. Watch for full-size masks, with all the bells and whistles: patent dates from the 19th century, throat protectors, visors, forehead pads, little side pads wired to the cage instead of laced, pointed fronts, early bead welds, etc. These are the masks most sought.

Spitters come next, being quite common and made popular by all the big league catchers of the 1930s. Watch for player endorsements here as they really add value.

Prewar masks without the spitters come next. Only buy top-of-the-line, pro quality and condition here. These are common and without a player endorsement and in top condition, they offer minimal collector potential. Loads of masks were donated to the war effort (1941-45) and are found marked with dates and branch of service. This does not affect listed values.

Postwar (1945) masks remain extremely common and are not collected except for use in displays or if they have a player endorsement such as Mantle or Berra. The padding snaps to the cage on postwar models and styles.

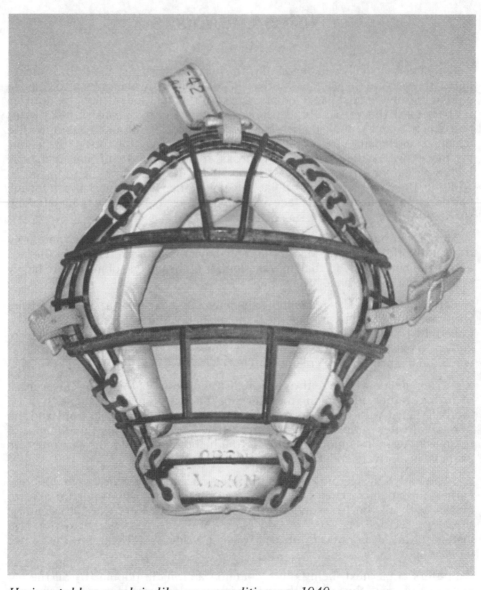

Horizontal bar mask in like new condition ca. 1940s.

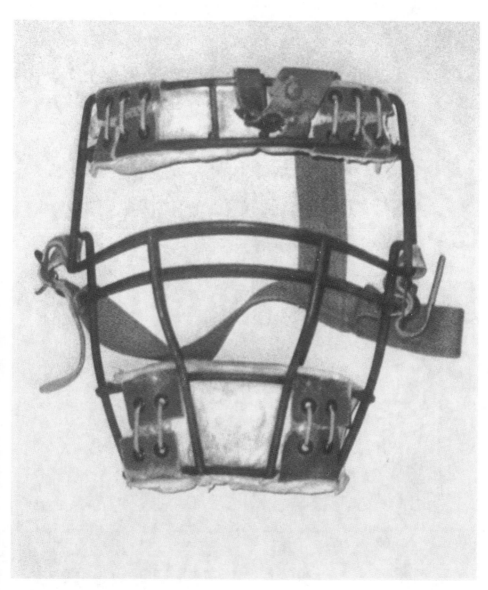

Typical softball mask ca. 1940-50.

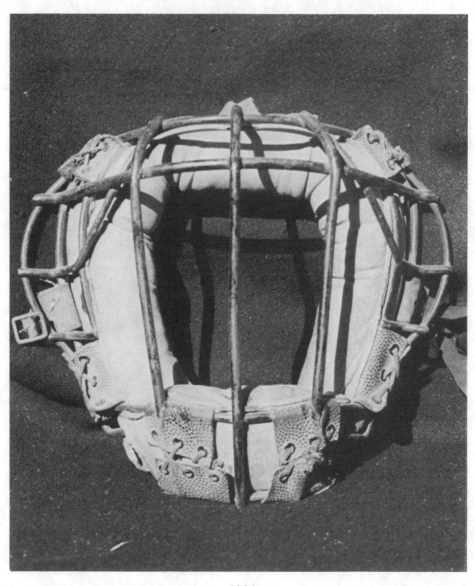

Strange three-bar vertical mask ca. 1930s.

Grading

Fair/poor - Rusty with metal worn through in spots, pads gone, wires missing. Dented badly, leather rotted. Headgear gone. Unless it's a Howland or a Thayer mask, or the intricacy of the metal is especially intriguing, stay away.

Good - Headgear missing or tied to cage. Metal rusty but all pieces there. Most pads present but dangling or stuffing sticking out. Small dents and pieces of metal separated at joint. Traces of rust but no corrosion.

Very Good - Headgear present but may be tied to mask. All pads intact without stuffing showing. Metal clean. Small dents, no metal separation. Tags missing.

Excellent - Headgear still attached in at least two of three locations. Leather soft. No rust, most original enamel present (a finish not found on all masks, look in hidden areas to determine if this applies), with most wear on high spots. No dents or metal separation. Partial tagging (if applicable).

Near Mint - Headgear perfect, any tags 100% complete, 90% or better metal finish, no dents, no rust. Padding perfect and attached in all spots.

Mint - An unused mask, never worn. Everything near perfect but allow for minor shelf wear on older models.

Price Guide

For boxes add:
Pre-1900 - at least 100%
1900-20 - at least 50%
1920-45 - 40%

Postwar through 1960s - at least 50%. This makes an unwanted mask collectible.

If box features pictures of player, it may command several times the value of the mask, depending on player and age.

Tags should add at least 30% to any prewar model, 10% on postwars.

Mint condition - add 40-50% on pre-1920 models, 30-40% on 1920-45 models, and 10% on postwar issues.

Deduct at least 50% on any child size masks or those with extremely thin wire (sandlot models). Early child masks tend to have an elastic head strap that goes horizontally across the back of the head with no strap over the top. Most full-size, professional quality masks will have headgear over the top.

MODEL	V.G.	EXC.	NR/MT	SUPPLY
Thayer or Howland	$800	$1300	$1800	rare

Spider mask (full-size), with hook or (+) clip connections.

MODEL	V.G.	EXC.	NR/MT	SUPPLY
With small pads	$150	$300	$450	varies
W/bead weld connections	$250	$500	$750	rare
W/full pads, laced	$125	$250	$375	common

Sun visor, either model add $25
Throat protector, either model add $150
Extended straps, add $50
Pre-1910 patent dates stamped, add $50

Note: To figure the price of masks with several features or mint condition: First, add any percentages to listed price (i.e. for mint boxes, tags, etc.), then add the dollar amounts listed for each special feature to arrive at a total price.

Early umpire model with throat protection as well as hinged ear protection.

	V.G.	EXC.	NR/MT	SUPPLY
	$150	$300	$450	rare
Prewar spitter	$50	$125	$200	common
Facsimile signature endorsements				
Hall of fame	$1-200	$2-300	$3-500	varies
Stars	$50-100	$1-200	$2-350	varies
Prewar non-spitter	$40	$80	$120	common

(If a non-spitter style has a player endorsement, deduct 10% off listed player models.)

Prewar composition metal solid bar masks, early models with padding laced to cage

	V.G.	EXC.	NR/MT	SUPPLY
	$50	$125	$200	common
Postwar, padding snapped	$20	$40	$60	common
Facsimile signature endorsements				
Hall of Fame	$40	$80	$120	varies
Stars	$20	$40	$60	varies

(Postwar models may be either solid bar or wire construction.)
(Softball masks have no collector value.)
(Half masks covering only the eyes are eyeglass protectors, usually used in basketball or handball. They will be priced in a later chapter.)

D & M Baseball Shoes

No. DB16—Kangaroo Uppers. Sprint Last. Goodyear stitched taps and heels. A very substantial shoe that will give good service. Genuine blue back kangaroo uppers, outside counter pockets, stitched shank. Semi-pro type spikes. Sizes 3 to 12 inclusive. Carried in stock in E width   Per Pair—$7.00

No. DB17—Sprint Last. "Sportan" leather uppers, oak leather taps and heels, outside counter pockets. Semi-pro type steel toe and heel spikes. Sizes 3 to 12 inclusive. Carried in stock in E width   Per Pair—$5.25

No. DB18—Sprint Last. A medium, low-priced shoe that will give exceptionally good service. "Sportan" leather uppers, oak soles. Semi-pro type steel toe and heel plates. Sizes 3 to 12 inclusive. Carried in stock in E width.   Per Pair—$4.60

D & M Baseball Masks

No. D267—Open Vision Style, Sunshade Model. Clear vision padding. Wide ear protecting frame, made of dull finished, heavy reinforced steel wire with welded joints. Soft leather, well-padded, clear vision face, head and chin cushions laced to frame. Adjustable elastic and web head straps.
Each—$6.65

No. D264—Open Vision Frame. Clear vision face padding. Full size, clear vision, soft leather face, head and chin cushions laced to frame. Wide ear protecting, black enameled, heavy steel wire frame with welded joints. Adjustable, elastic and web head straps   Each—$5.65

No. D254—Youth's Mask. Open vision style, black enameled steel wire frame, welded joints. Padded leather face, head and chin cushion laced to frame. Elastic strap   Each—$3.25

No. DB16

No. DB17

No. DB18

No. D267

No. D264

No. D254

Baseball Bases

No. D0—Extra heavy bleached duck, firmly stuffed. Quilted top. Extra heavy, 4-ply braided canvas strap with hand-forged wrought steel spikes   Per Set of 3—$9.00

No. D0

No. D1

No. D1—Heavy bleached duck. Plain top. Complete with strap through leather tunnel opening, and spike.
Per Set of 3—$6.60

No. D2—Bleached duck, not stuffed. Plain top with laced opening   Per Set of 3—$3.00

Sliding Pads

No. D8—Eddie J. Roush "No Bruise" Pad. Made of two layers of quilted, padded white drill with binding. Ties around waist and leg, elastic back. Light weight, this pad will not bind   Each—$2.45

No. D3—Made of quilted, padded white drill with reinforcement over hips. Ties at waist, elastic back. An inexpensive, light weight model.
Each—$2.00

No. D8

No. D3

Prices Subject to Change Without Notice.

—7—

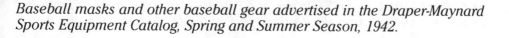

Baseball masks and other baseball gear advertised in the Draper-Maynard Sports Equipment Catalog, Spring and Summer Season, 1942.

No. M13 Front   No. M13 Back   No. M12

No. M10

No. M9

No. M8

No. M7

BASE BALL GOODS

USED BY ALL THE LEADING PLAYERS

D&M

THE MOST RELIABLE AND STRONGEST MADE

HANK GOWDY

"The Lucky Dog Kind"

20

Two pages from a 1922 Spring and Summer D & M catalog featuring spiderman catcher's masks. Notice some of the features such as the throat

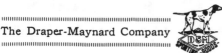
D. & M. Catchers' Masks

No. M13   Hank Gowdy's Mask. We were talking to Hank the other day and he said he was using the same mask that he bought when he first played base ball after the war. There is several years' good, hard service for a mask and it is a recommendation. He said it was in just as good shape as it ever was. This Mask is a big, fairly heavy, double wire affair — a typical protection for the man who is in constant service behind the bat.   Price............$8.00

No. M12.   This is Bill Killifer's model — so called because we first made it for him. This is made of heavy single wire with a wide-open vision frame; has ear protections; continuous hair-filled pad and heavy chin cushion which protects the wearer from shock, the same as on the M13.   Price.... 7.00

No. M10.   An open-vision, spitter model with double-wire frame.   Full-length hair-stuffed side pads. Molded leather forehead and chin strap and has extension neck protection as shown in the cut.   Price............ 7.00

No. M9.   Heavy wire, open-vision, spitter model. Continuous hair-stuffed pad. Black sole leather sun shade. Price................... 5.00

No. M8.   Open-vision, spitter model, continuous hair-filled pad.. 4.25

No. M7.   Open-vision, sun-shaded Mask with large hair-filled pads... 4.00

No. M6.   Open-vision, hair-filled pad. Molded leather head and chin pieces. Price... 3.00

No. M5.   Large size, well padded. Leather head and chin pieces.. 2.25

No. M4.   A Boys' Mask with continuous hair-stuffed pad.   Price.. 2.00

No. M3.   Boys' Mask. Stuffed pad. Leather head and chin pieces. Price... 1.50

No. M2.   Boys' Mask. Well padded. Equipped with head and chin pieces. Price.. 1.25

No. M1.   Boys' Mask. Well padded. Price.................. 1.00

No. M4   No. M5   No. M6

All D. & M. Masks are made with electrically welded joints making the strongest possible construction. They are a real protection — not simply little wire cages made to sell, but they are made to protect the man behind the bat, than whom there is not a man on the team that needs more protection.

protection and flat forehead piece on item M10. Built-in leather sun visors are apparent on items M12 and M13.

161

REACH CATCHERS' MASKS

ALL Masks on this page are made of heavy steel wire, gun metal enameled to prevent reflection of light, and are fitted with moulded leather chin straps, special full length "patented" hair-filled leather side pads, head pad and elastic head bands.

A new idea in mask construction The center wire is omitted enabling the catcher to see much clearer; in fact as well as if he had no mask on.
No. WS with sunshade **Each**
. . . . **$6.00**
No. OE? without sunshade **Each**
. . . . **$5.00**

No. SL. Made of extra heavy wire, gun metal enameled, well brazed joints, extra strong.
Each **$5.00**

No. 6W. Double extra wire, black enameled. Extra well padded . . . . **Each $6.00**

No. 00. Made of extra heavy wire, fitted with leather sunshade. Extra well padded. **Each $4.00**
No. 400 New wide sight mask, extra strong black wire, padded with our patented pads. A great mask at the price.
Each **$4.00**

No. 10S. Heavy wire, black enameled. Well padded neck protecting-piece. **Each** . **$4.00**
No. 0S. Same as No. 10S, but without sunshade. **Each $3.50**
No. 20S. Same as No. 10S, but without neckpiece. **Each** . . **$3.00**
No. 1S. Same as No. 20S, but without sunshade. **Each $2.50**

"Association" Mask, made of heavy steel wire. Special side and head pads.
No. 30S. With sunshade **Each**
. . . . **$2.50**
No. 2S. Without sunshade **Each**
. . . . **$2.00**
No. 40S. Regulation Mask, similar to No. 30S. **Each** . **$2.00**

Heavy steel wire, black enameled, well padded. Fitted with patent transparent sunshade.
No. 50S. . . . . **Each $1.5·**
No. 60S. Junior size **Each $1.5**

No. CM. Youths' Mask. Heavy wire, no head or chin piece. **Each** . . . **$0.50**

No. DM. Youths' Mask. Light wire, no head or chin piece. **Each** . . . **$0.25**

No. 25S. Amateur Mask. Full size, heavy wire, black enameled . . . . **Each $1.50**

Umpires Ma

No. XX. Lighter wire. **Each** **$1.00**
No. XS. Same as XX but youths size. **Each** **$1.00**
No. 3M. Similar to XS, but without head padding
Each **$0.75**

No. 4U. Special neck and ear protecting atta· ments. **Each** . . . . **$5.·**
No. 3U. Same, without neck protector.
Each **$4.50**

Baseball masks and other baseball gear advertised in the Draper-Maynard Sports Equipment Catalog, Spring and Summer Season, 1942.

CHEST PROTECTORS

Chest protectors appeared on the scene soon after the advent of the catcher's mask, sometime during the 1880s. The need to protect one's body became apparent after the realization of the benefits to life and limb offered by the relatively new catcher's mask. Not only catchers, but plate umpires also realized the advantages of body protection, and they too, adopted the chest protectors as well as the masks.

But what makes a chest protector collectible? How many different models were made? What do you do with them?

Well, the answers to the above questions are as varied as the people who collect them. Combined with a mask, shinguards, and a glove, the catcher's outfit is one of the more desirable displays at sports bars and restaurants. Early style chest protectors are extremely scarce and yet are usually quite affordable when found. As to models, there were dozens of slight differences in regards to sizes, shapes, and shades as retailed by the various manufacturers, but they still remain quite similar in appearance to their early, nineteenth century counterparts. When discussing prewar (1945) and postwar styles, the most common delineation remains the "crotch protector," that small section of protector that hangs below the waist when a catcher is in position and protects the body below the belt. The advent of better protective cups and the added advantage of mobility offered by the postwar waist-high style led to the demise of the crotch protector. Obviously, this design shift didn't happen on the first day of 1946, nor did all the manufacturers change at the same time. And even then, most of the old designs were re-used in the less expensive lines, or child's models. It is not unusual to find a protection model in blue or orange from the 1950s in a smaller child size. Most prewar canvas models will have piping much like a baseball glove. This piping or edging will be found either laced completely with rawhide around the perimeter or sewn. In either case, the leather piping will always be the more desirable, and professional, than those with the plastic piping.

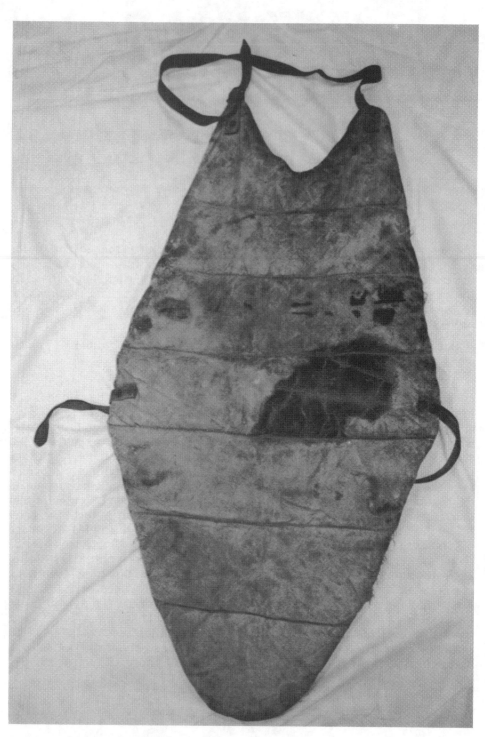

Leather protector ca. 1890s.

Glossary

Inflated model - This is the style favored by catchers at the turn of the century. Made of rubber and covered in cotton or canvas, the bladder would be inflated with air through a fill nozzle much like those found on automobile tires.

Belted model - The word belted refers to the center or waist belt, sewn to the front of early protectors. It resembles the inflated models, but is padded with felt or horsehair, and then covered in heavy cotton or other strong material. A similar model may be found without the sewn belt on the front. Neither the belted nor the inflated model have the low-hanging crotch protection and are rounded at the bottom.

Quilted model - This model, another popular model dating from the late nineteenth century through the teens, was made of heavy felt or horsehair with the heavy cotton or canvas outer covering quilted in approximately two inch diamonds or squares.

Prewar model - This refers to the models made from the mid-teens through the war years (1941-45). Made of heavy canvas, usually in O.D. (olive drab) or tan, with or without a leather bottom section. Will also be found made of all leather but extremely scarce in that style. Easily distinguishable by the low hanging crotch protection discussed earlier.

Postwar style - Made of O.D. or tan canvas, this model is cut off at the waist and is rounded at that point. There is no extended protection below that point.

Straps - Made of leather or canvas or both, this refers to the system of belts and buckles (metal adjusters) on the back of chest protectors. Completeness of straps is integral to collector value.

Umpire's model - Used by umpires, these models were often inflatable, wider at the shoulders than a catcher's model and usually lacking the crotch protection piece. Generally broad and short and easily distinguishable from a catcher's model.

Endorsed model - This model will be found bearing the stamped facsimile autograph or block letter name of a famous catcher or player. Usually found stamped in the upper torso section, an endorsement will always add value to a protector.

Reed model - A style popular during the teens, it is usually found in O.D. (olive drab) or tan canvas with wooded doll rods running vertically underneath as the major form of protection. This style or design is the same as that found in reed shinguards, both baseball and football.

Late postwar models - These are the models found in an array of colors such as orange, blue, black, red, or a combination. These late models have little collector value or interest unless they bear the stamped endorsement of a famous player, and even then, the value will be nominal.

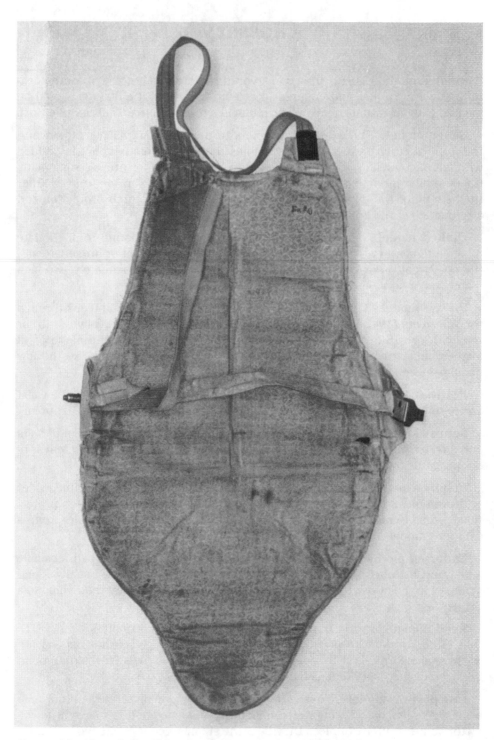

Strap side of an inflatable chest protector ca. 1890-1910.

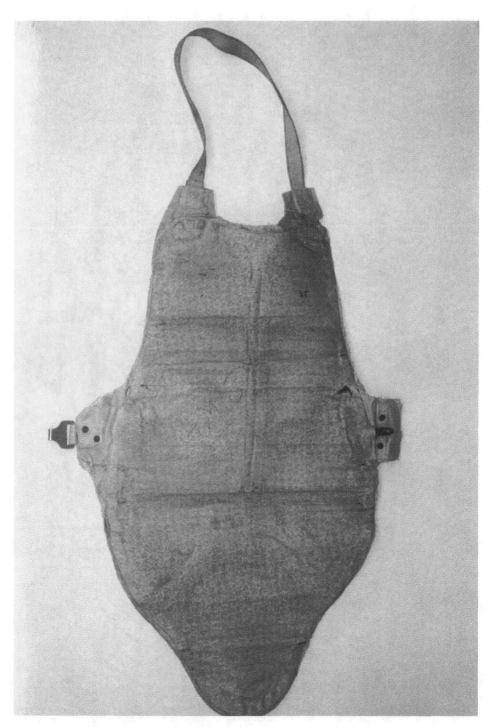

Face side of inflatable chest protector showing metal air valve ca. 1890-1910.

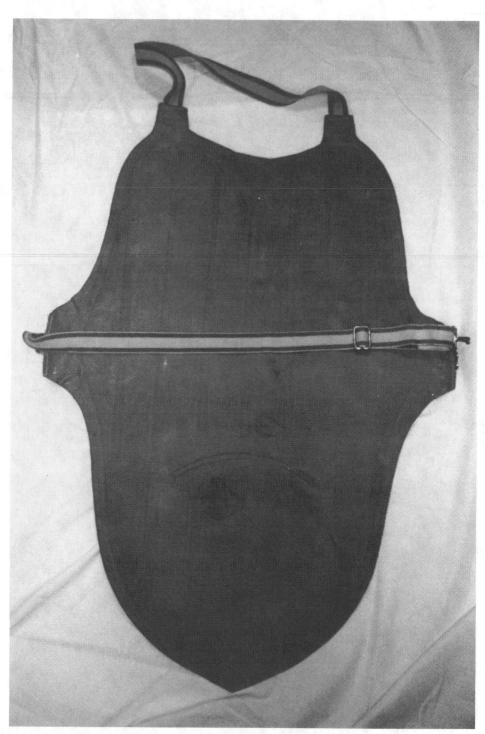

D & M inflatable chest protector ca. 1890-1910.

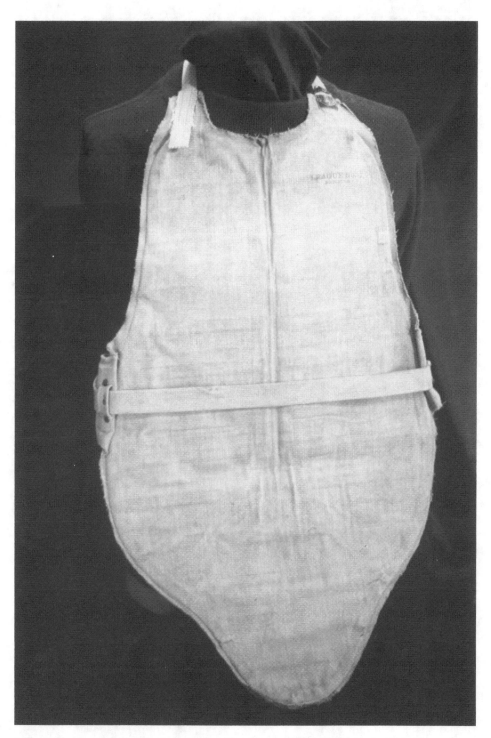

Inflatable outside belted chest protector ca. 1890-1910.

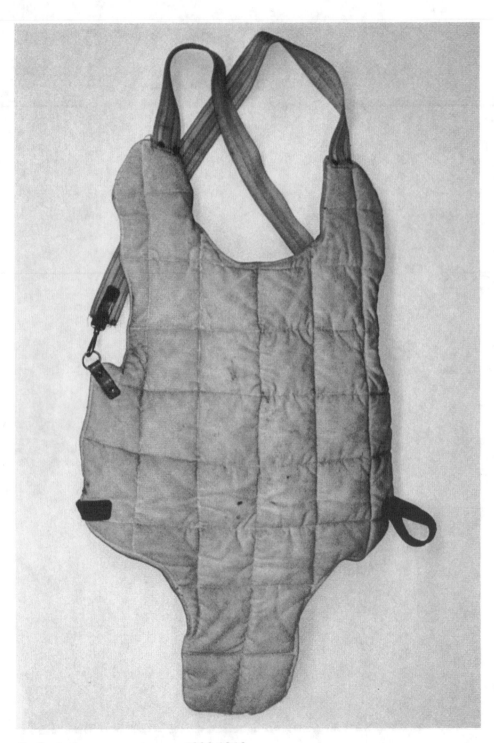

Quilted chest protector ca. 1890-1910.

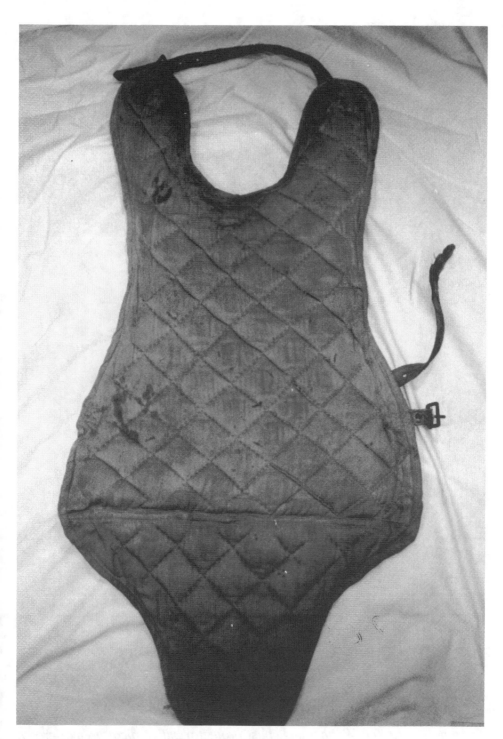

Diamond quilted chest protector ca. 1890-1910.

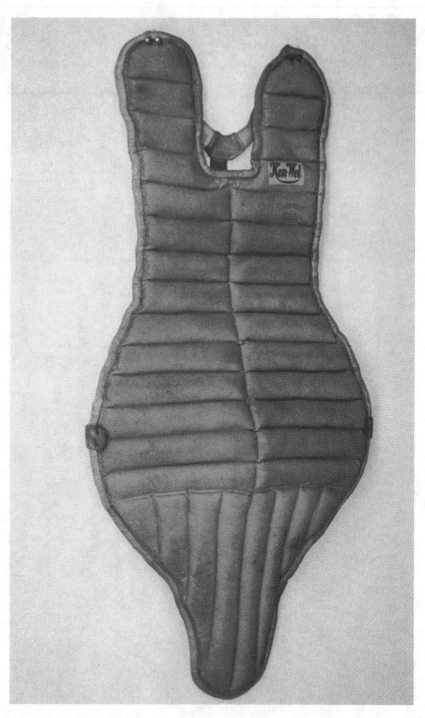

Extremely long Ken Wel canvas chest protector with typical prewar crotch extension ca. 1930.

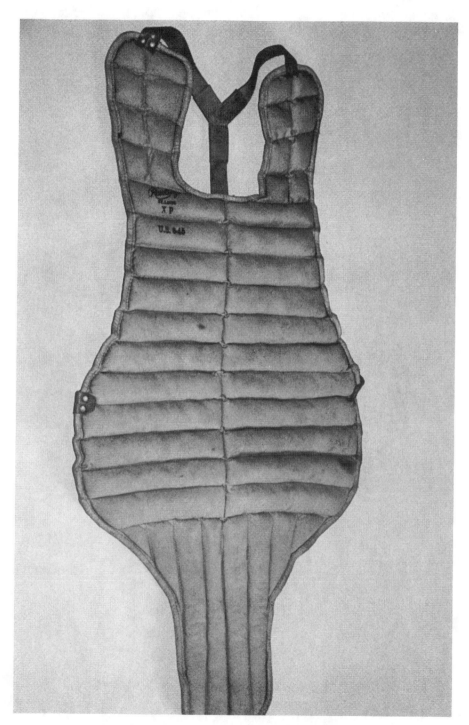

Elongated canvas chest protector marked 1945, a wartime government issue.

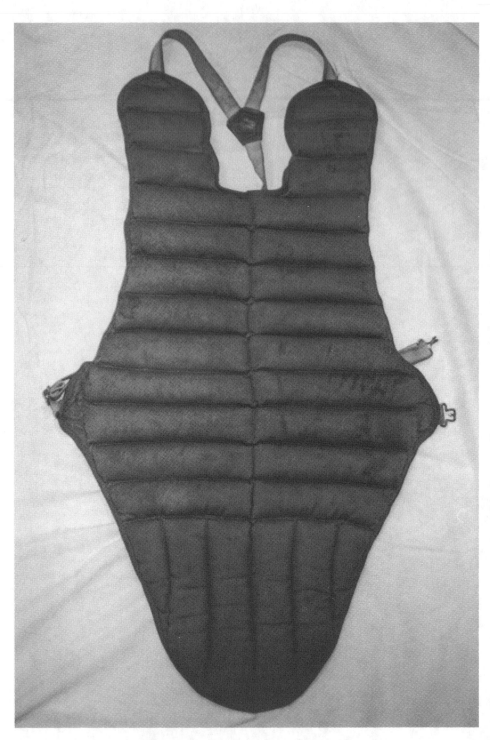

Canvas chest protector ca. 1900-20 with rounded base.

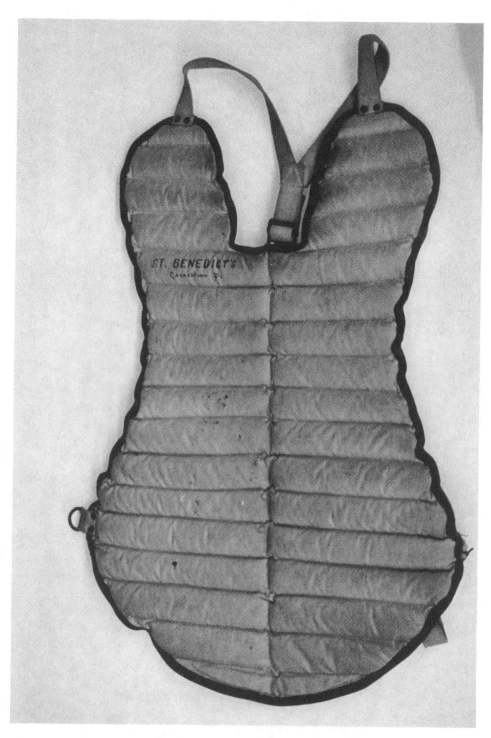

Canvas chest protector without extending crotch ca. 1940-50.

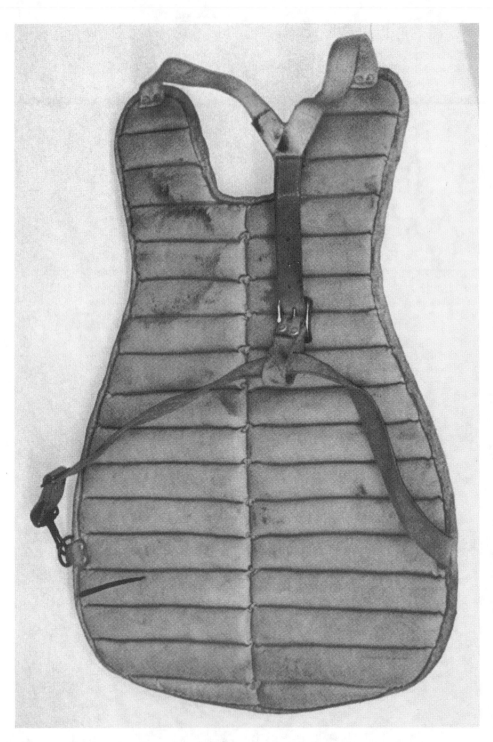

Strap or back side of a typical 1950s chest protector.

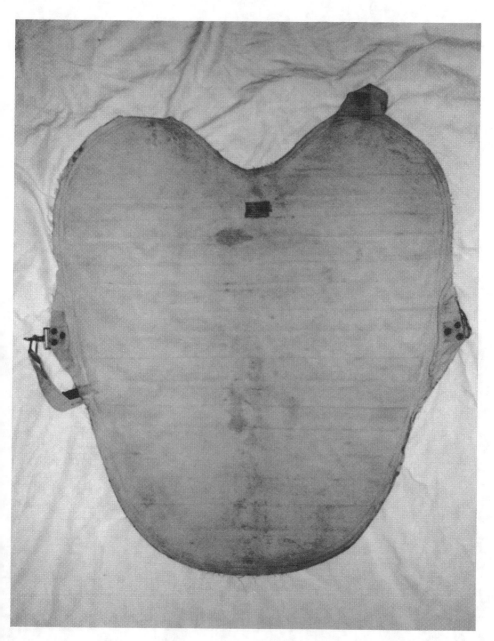

Inflatable umpire's chest protector ca. 1900-20.

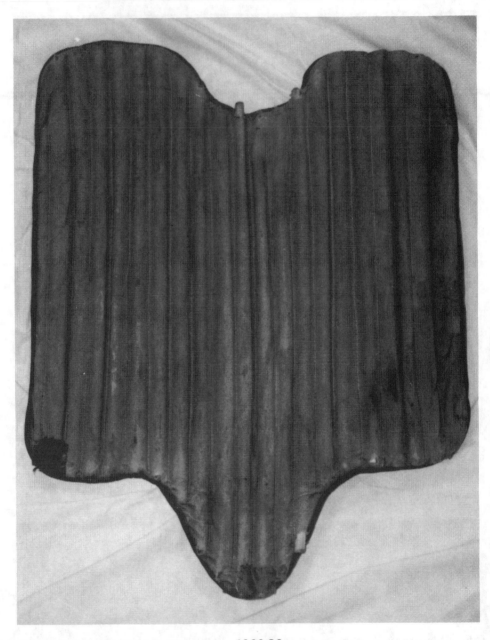

Goldsmith reed chest protector ca. 1900-20.

Grading

The grading of chest protectors is much like shinguards. Straps are important to value, as is piping. Early styles will always be more desirable in any grade while later models will be hard sells unless in top condition. Collectors are much more forgiving, in regards to condition, on earlier and scarcer items.

Fair/poor - Straps gone, large holes and tears, severe staining or writing on face, stuffing exposed, piping badly worn and gone in spots.

Good - General soiling or spotting, some straps still attached, small holes or tears, piping worn in spots. No writing on face.

Very Good - Minor soiling or concentrated spotting, all straps intact but buckles or adjustments may be missing or rusted, small holes but sparse without tearing, no writing, any tags still intact and readable. Piping worn but complete.

Excellent - Clean with no holes or tears, all straps intact and adjustments working, no writing, piping strong with only minor edge wear, all tags. Any inflatable chest protector must still hold some air to be rated with this grade. If you have a strong inflatable model in all respects but it will not take or hold air, grade accordingly.

Near Mint - No holes or tears, all straps perfect, no writing, piping like new, all tags perfect. Inflatable models with perfect rubber bladders and nozzles.

Mint - As new, regardless of age. Never used.

Price Guide

Boxed add:
Pre-1900 - (at least 100%)
1900-20 - (at least 50%)
1920-45 - (40%)
Postwar - (20%)

Boxes displaying a picture of a player will increase value at least 100%, maybe several times the listed value depending on player.

Child models, deduct 30% on prewar models and 50% or more on postwar models. (Basically, postwar child models are not collectible except as decorator items.)

TYPE	V.G.	EXC.	NR/MT	SUPPLY
Inflatable	$200	$350	$500	rare
Umpire (prewar)	$100	$200	$300	rare

WILSON BASEBALL EQUIPMENT

Wilson Catchers' and Umpires' Protectors

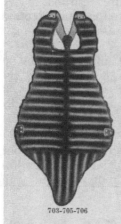

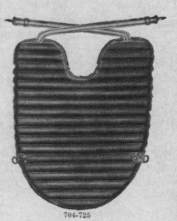

705. Professional Catchers' Protector, heavy army duck, tan color, padded with highest quality Java Kapok, leather bound, elastic shoulder straps, adjustable leather back straps. (Not inflated)....................**Each, $7.50**
706. Regulation Catchers' Protector, tan color duck with curled hair padding, leather bound, elastic shoulder straps, adjustable leather back straps. (Not inflated)..............**Each, $5.50**
703. Boys' Catcher's Protector, tan color duck, curled hair padding, elastic shoulder straps, adjustable web back straps. (Not inflated)......**Each, $3.50**
No. 704. Umpires' Heavy army duck, padded with Java Kapok. Leather binding; adjustable elastic shoulder straps. Not inflated................**Each, $7.50**
No. 725. Umpires' Inflated. Pure rubber, covered with the best quality canvas. Held in position by adjustable web straps................**Each, $17.00**

703-705-706

704-725

Wilson Leg Guards

722   723   702   724   700-701

No. 722. Wilson "Patented Take-Down" Umpires' and Catchers' Leg Guards, made in three sections. Can be carried in traveling bag or uniform roll. Leg section aluminum; knee cap and foot guard finest quality heavy chocolate cowhide, felt lined. All sections shaped properly and give absolute protection..**Pair, $12.00**
723. Catchers' Leg Guard, curved fibre shin pieces, moulded fibre knee caps, felt lined; felt lined leather covered hinge at knee, fibre extension over instep with foam rubber padding; adjustable straps..**Pair, $10.00**
No. 702. Leg sections covered with strong moulded fibre and with leather knee cap. All sections joined together by good quality leather. Very durable and light in weight......................**Per Pair, $8.00**

724. Umpires' Leg Guard, narrow curved fibre shin pieces, moulded leather knee caps, felt lined; with leather hinge at knee, felt lined leather covered ankle protectors, adjustable straps. Worn under clothing.
Pair, $8.00

No. 700. Professional Model. Knee cap of heavy leather, lined with felt. Flexible joint just below knee allowing freedom of action. Leg section of excellent quality strong white leather....**Per Pair, $7.50**

No. 701. Identical with No. 700 model, except white canvas used in leg section instead of white leather.
Per Pair, $6.00

30

Examples of Catchers' and Umpires' Protectors taken from the Wilson Athletic Equipment Spring & Summer Catalog, 1932.

TYPE	V.G.	EXC.	NR/MT	SUPPLY
Umpire (postwar)	$40	$80	$120	common
Ump (not inflated)	$20	$40	$60	common
Quilted	$150	$300	$450	rare
Prewar canvas	$60	$100	$150	common
Prewar leather	$100	$200	$300	rare

Leather refers to all leather or bottom half leather models. On canvas models above, deduct 10-20% for plastic piping.

Reed model	$100	$200	$300	rare

Prewar endorsed models

Hall of Fame	$100	$200	$300	varies
Stars	$75	$150	$250	varies

Any pre-1920 stars or Hofers, add at least 30% to above prices.

Postwar endorsed models

Hall of Fame	$50	$75	$100	varies
Stars	$25	$50	$75	varies

Postwar non-endorsed models

O.D. or tan canvas	$25	$50	$75	common
Blue, orange, etc.	$10	$20	$30	common

Front View   **Back View**

No. CP   Each $2.50

The Reach "Patented" Body Protector No. CP, made of Heavy Canvas, with Heavy Reeds to break the Force of Blow. Laced in Back (see illustration). This forms an air chamber, making an absolute protection for the catcher. Will outwear the inflated protector and will prevent injury to the one using it.

No. 2P Each $1.50

The Reach Men's Body Protector No. 2P, made of Heavy Canvas, with Heavy Reeds, to break the force of Blow. Padded with Best Felt. Postage, 25c. extra.

No.   Each
3P $1.00

The Reach Boys' Body Protector No. 3P, made of Heavy Canvas, Padded with Best Felt. A thorough protection for the catcher. Postage, 20c extra.

GRAY PATENT PROTECTORS, the only practical device for the protection of catchers and umpires. They are made of the best rubber, inflated with air, light and pliable, and do not interfere with the movements of the wearer under any conditions. When not in use the air may be let out and the protector rolled in a very small space.

BEWARE of Inferior Quality Inflated Body Protectors. Buy only the BEST, they bear the REACH Trade-Mark—All grades. They are GUARANTEED.

No.   Each
15P Umpire $12.00

The Reach Inflated Umpire's Body Protector. Easily put on and taken off. It protects every part of the body that needs protection. Patented November 24, 1903

We have had numerous inquiries from umpires for a BODY PROTECTOR that would THOROLY protect.

This led us to design one which we guarantee will protect the wearer from the hardest blows and at the same time not interfere with his movements.

Special Umpire Body Protectors made to order. Write for particulars and prices.

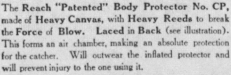

We are the ORIGINATORS of all the PRACTICAL DESIGNS and IDEAS that are embodied in CATCHERS' MITTS, FIRST BASEMEN'S MITTS, FIELDERS' MITTS and GLOVES; they are endorsed by all the leading professional and amateur players.

31

Reed and Inflatable Models of Catchers' and Umpires' Protectors, A.J. Reach Company 1909 Season Catalog.

SHINGUARDS

Shinguards had been used by football and cricket players long before New York Giants' catcher and future Hall of Famer Roger Bresnahan wore them in major league play against Fred Clarke's Pirates in 1907. Like anything new introduced to baseball, its players, and fans, the shinguards, and Roger Bresnahan, were heartily jeered. However, by the following winter, they met with the approval of the league and the rest is history.

Baseball shinguards have been made in a variety of styles since their inception on the major league diamonds. These include reed shins and buckskins, some with protection for the top of the feet, others without. Even after all of these years, aside from the material used, they remain virtually unchanged. Shinguards were not popular in the beginning. The 1909 Reach catalog doesn't even list them and the 1913 Victor catalog lists only the Umpires' Leg Guards "made of choice harness leather and felt lining. Special cupped knee...allows easy use of the leg while removing every element of danger." But it wasn't long before industry caught up with the demand.

Today early shinguards may be one of the most difficult items to add to your collection of catcher's gear. Reeded shins, ones in which actual wooden dolls are surrounded by canvas or buckskin and run from the knee pad to the ankle, are the most highly coveted. Also available were the leg guards made of molded fiber, smooth faced, with metal rivets holding the inner leather to the fiber. This in turn kept the leg guards rounded in the front. The fiber material tends to return to its original flat shape once the inside leather has pulled away from the rivets, and that is why so many molded fiber shins exist in their flattened shape. Most shinguards of this period offered some sort of knee protection, either of the same material as the rest of the shin or of plain felt (which didn't last long).

During this period, some companies started to offer shinguards endorsed by famous catchers, a practice now being used on all pieces of equipment. Famous players' names helped sell items, and catcher's gear was no exception. Reach offered their Mickey Cochrane Leg Guards while McGregor Goldsmith carried the Bill Dickey line. Facsimile autographs are commonly found in the leather that separates the knee pad from the shinguard itself and usually can be found on both pieces.

By the late 1930s, the smooth-faced molded fiber leg guards were becoming a thing of the past. The reeded models became unpopular during the late 1920s. A new style of shinguard appeared "made of corrugated fibre." This new style of guard had horizontal ridges running across the shin and all models offered the foot protection for the instep. These models remained the same until the new plastics outdated them during the mid to late 1950s.

Even though there are a multitude of makers and subtle differences in most shinguards, there are only a few categories as to pricing and collectible status.

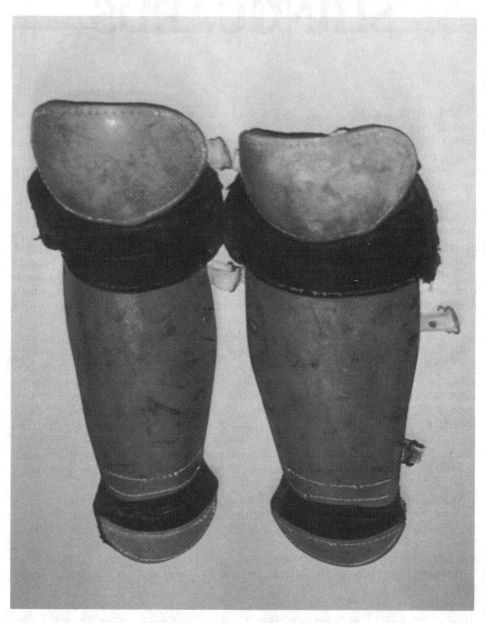

Top view of ca. 1920 smooth-face shinguards with contrasting black leather hinges.

Glossary

Shinguards - Apparatus used since 1907 to protect the catcher's legs and knees.

Reeds - Wooded doll rods running the length between the knee and the top of foot or instep. Their form is visible but they are encased in leather or canvas. Reed models will have felt or leather knee pads and a piece of leather at the base that is either cut out for the top of the foot or they will have a piece of leather covering the instep.

Umpire's leg guards - Similar to catcher's guards except narrow to allow them to be worn under loose fitting pants. They often have their straps across the front of the leg guard, but not always.

Straps - These are the leather or canvas straps at the back of the shinguards that attach to the catcher's legs. The usual early buckle system for tightening resembled the old snaps on galoshes. Later shinguards had the pull-through adjustments.

Knee pad - The leather or felt section protecting the knee. It will be found connected to the rest of the shin by pliable leather allowing bending and freedom of movement.

Instep - This is the covering found at the base of the shinguard, also attached to the leg area with leather. This piece, not always found on early guards, protected the top of the catcher's foot.

Grading

Fair/Good - Leather rotted, straps gone, holes in fibre or canvas. Reeds sticking out or missing. Inside leather gone or busted out, shape gone.

Very Good - Leather thin in spots or stiff. Some of straps still attached. All reeds intact but visible through holes in canvas. Insides are there but pulled away from rivets, shape gone. Heavy scuffing on leather with rough finish.

Excellent - Leather pliable. Most straps and buckles still attached and operable. No holes in canvas, no reeds exposed. Insides not pulled away. Round shape remains. Minor scuffing and scratches. No major gouges in outside leather.

Near Mint - Leather still soft. All straps attached and operable. No holes or tears. Insides intact with all shape remaining. Playable if needed. No gouges and only the slightest scuffing from use.

Mint - As always, like new. No scuffing at all. Never used in a game.

Prewar umpire shinguards–thin models with front straps going across face.

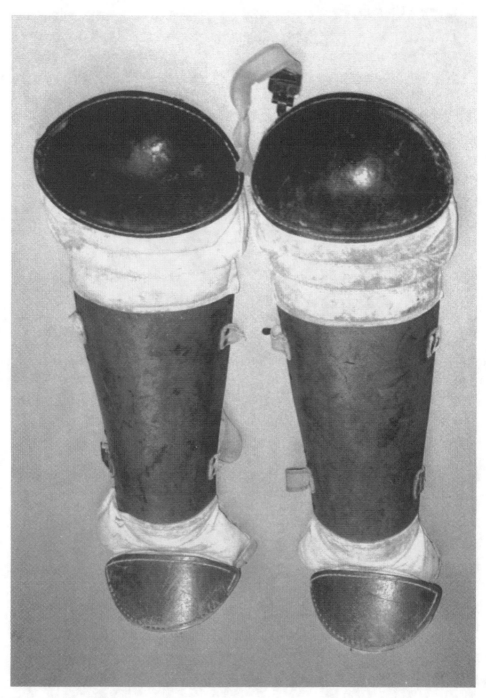

Prewar shinguards with white buckskin connecting leather, black leather kneepads, and smooth faced.

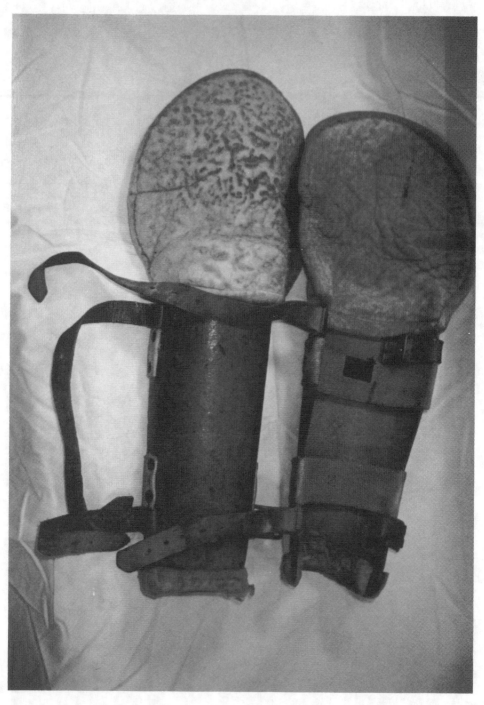

Unusual shinguards with only the felt covering the knees and no leather ca. 1910-20.

Typical prewar shinguards with smooth face, leather inner supports and canvas straps ca. 1920-40.

Reeded shinguards of white canvas over wooden reeds with leather knee pads ca. 1910-20.

Reeded shinguards made of white buckskin covering wooden reeds and black leather kneepads ca. 1910-20.

Close-up of ca. 1920s umpire shinguards. Notice outside straps across face.

Smooth-face shinguards ca. 1920-30.

Price Guide

Add 50% to near-mint price on reeds and smooth composition fibre.

Add 25% to near-mint price on horizontal ridged corrugated fibre.

Boxes for any shinguards are extremely scarce. Add at least 50% to mint price for any nice box. As always, one picturing a famous player would add even greater value.

For colors of smooth shins other than brown, add 20%.

For reeded shins covered in white buckskin, add 20%.

Unusual colors, if factory, on prewar shinguards will add value as well.

TYPE	V.G.	EXC.	NR/MT	SUPPLY
Reeded shins	$250	$450	$650	scarce
Smooth composition	$125	$250	$350	common
Signature models for above				
Hall of fame reeds	$350	$600	$850	
Star players reeds	$300	$500	$800	
(No known example of above signature models.)				
HOF composition	$200	$400	$600	scarce
Star players composition	$175	$350	$500	scarce
Prewar umpires shins	$50	$100	$150	common
Corrugated fibre	$50	$75	$125	common
Prewar players (Fiber)				
HoF players (Fiber)	$100	$150	$200	varies
Stars (Fiber)	$75	$125	$175	varies
Postwar players				
HoF players	$75	$125	$175	varies
Star players	$50	$75	$125	varies

Plastic shinguards are not collectible at present except as decorations unless they have endorsements.

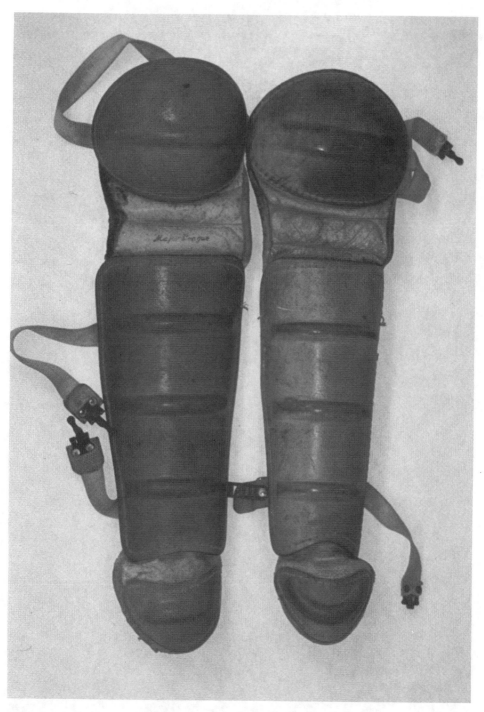

Front view of typical pair of ca. 1940-50 horizontal ridge composition shinguards.

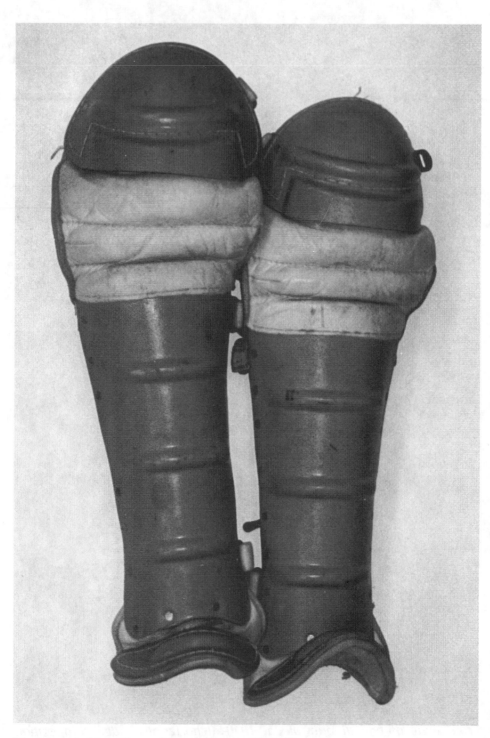

Horizontal ridged-face shinguards ca. 1940-50.

UNIFORMS

Ever since the first warriors went into battle, the need arose to identify the feuding factions. Uniforms were created to serve this purpose. They offered the participant and viewer alike the ability to determine who was on what side. Uniforms became the proud symbol of what a group represented or from where they hailed. Like a flag, a uniform was a source of pride. In essence, it represented who we were. In wars, people would shed their blood and that of others based solely on the flag they followed and the uniform they wore. Uniforms were loud and boisterous or subdued. They were rigid and formal or loose and comfortable, but they still represented the same things–ideals and camaraderie. The uniform became an essential part of the game of baseball. It imposed the delineation of friend and foe, home team and visitor.

In 1869, the Mutual Nine of New York wore natty uniforms that resembled naval personnel, with an elastic and leather belt emblazoned with the team name. Others, like the 1859 Atwater Club, wore white tunics under a sailor-like jersey with bow ties. Still others wore matching white shirts and ties; others wore vests and jackets.

The first really popular style of baseball tunic was called the bib front, similar to those jerseys already in use by the United States cavalry and firefighters. It was a jersey with a collar and a separate removable section, much like a bib that buttoned to the shirt from both sides. On these bib fronts were embroidered, or sewn, the team's initials.

Bib front jerseys and those that followed will be covered in this chapter. Since this section deals with uniforms, we will also discuss the early sporting belts, pants, and caps that were worn with the jerseys. This chapter, as with all others, deals only with generic uniforms as ordered through the various mail-order houses or purchased at one of the many new sporting good stores springing up around the country.

Glossary

Bib front jersey - One of the early, more popular styles of organized baseball teams. They found favor during the 1860s and 1870s. Called bib fronts because they are tunics that have a piece of material on the front that appears to be separate from the shirt, resembling a bib. They will usually be seen with a letter or symbol representing the team on the center of the bib. They were often worn with bow ties. They are extremely scarce today. Warning: watch for sporting labels such as Peck & Snyder, Reach, Spalding, etc., to avoid buying an early fireman's tunic.

Bib front jersey, no maker, ca. 1880s. Beware of fire department uniforms.

Lace-up front jersey with pill box cap ca. 1890-1910.

Lace-up front jersey with detachable sleeves and small bill cap ca. 1890-1910.

Collar style uniform with detachable sleeves, pill box cap, elastic and leather belt, and quilted pants ca. 1890-1910.

Collar style jersey ca. 1900-15.

Collar style uniform with pill box cap, elastic and leather belt ca. 1890-1910.

Lace up jersey - A style of jersey popular from the 1870s until the second decade of the century. This style has a shirt collar and laces up the front instead of having a bib or buttons. These too, are scarce but not as difficult to locate as a bib front. Most examples seen have a team name sewn on front.

Collar jersey - Spans the same time period as the lace-up jersey. It is identical, with the large shirt collar, except that it buttons up, usually half way, instead of the pullover lace-up style. Both the lace-up and button-up shirt collar jerseys were worn in the major leagues until 1911, the last year for the lace-up being 1910. The button-up shirt collar lasted until 1913, attesting to the enduring popularity of the two styles. It is this longevity that makes jerseys of these two styles easier to acquire than a bib front. The lace-up is still the more difficult to obtain of these two styles.

Cadet collar jersey (collar stands straight up) ca. 1905-15.

Cadet collar jersey - This style of jersey is reminiscent of the West Point cadet uniform. It is a short collar that stands straight up with a two to four inch gap in front. Some refer to them as the nehru collar after that style of shirt worn in the 1960s. Popular during the first two decades of this century, this style is fairly easy to locate today.

Sun collar jersey - This is the name given to the jerseys in which another small collar is sewn into the existing scoop collar. Popular from the middle of the first decade until late 1930s. Examples of this style are easy to locate.

Scoop collar - The above jersey without the small inner sewn collar. It too, appeared during the middle of the first decade and remained until the demise of flannel jerseys.

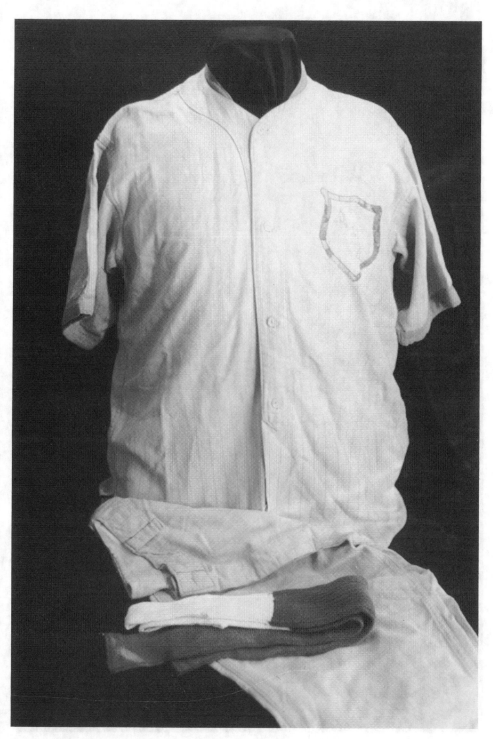

Sun collar uniform, (inner collar), ca. 1920s.

Sun collar uniform ca. 1920s-30s.

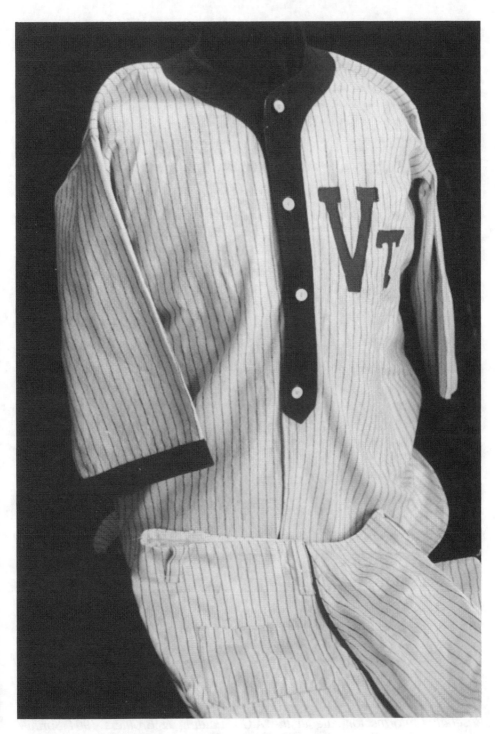

Town team uniform with standard collar and three-quarter sleeves ca. 1920-30.

BASE BALL

In base ball, as in other sports, the constant desire of every player is to excel his fellows. He cannot expect to do this unless his outfit is first-class and any disadvantage he is working under in this direction will detract just so much from ultimate results. For over a quarter of a century we have made the suits worn by the best players in this country, outfitting all the league clubs and colleges. To-day we are turning out uniforms which possess all the advantages made possible by our accumulated experience during that period, aided by a factory equipment second to none.

FRED CLARK
CAPTAIN PITTSBURG CLUB
NATIONAL LEAGUE

THE SPALDING UNIFORM NO. O Highest Grade Made

The workmanship and material of this outfit is of the very highest quality throughout and special care has been taken to make this uniform superior to anything offered in this line. Used exclusively by all league and professional clubs for years past is sufficient evidence of its quality and durability. Colors: White, Pearl Gray, Yale Gray, Light Gray, Black, Maroon, Royal Blue, Navy Blue, Brown, Green, Cardinal. The Spalding Shirt, any style; The Spalding Pants, any style; The Spalding Stockings, No. 3-0; The Spalding Cap, any style; The Spalding Web Belt, leather lined.

The Spalding Uniform, complete, $15.60

Net price to clubs ordering **$12.50** Detachable sleeves, 25 for **Entire Team**...Per suit cents each shirt, extra. No extra charge for lettering shirts with name of club.

THE UNIVERSITY UNIFORM No. 1

In workmanship and quality of material our University Uniform No. 1 is equal to our No. O Uniform, but slightly lighter. Colors: White, Pearl Gray, Yale Gray, Light Gray, Black, Maroon, Royal Blue, Navy Blue, Brown, Green, Cardinal. The University Shirt, any style; The University Pants, any style; The University Stockings, all wool, No. 1R; The University Cap, any style; The University Web Belt, or all leather.

The University Uniform, complete, $12.50

Net price to clubs ordering **$10.00** Detachable sleeves, 25 for **Entire Team**...Per suit cents each shirt, extra. No extra charge for lettering shirts with name of club.

THE INTERSCHOLASTIC UNIFORM No. 2

Made of same grade of material as our higher-priced uniforms, but of lighter weight flannel. Substantially made and a most serviceable outfit. Colors: White, Pearl Gray, Yale Gray, Light Gray, Black, Maroon, Royal Blue, Navy Blue, Brown, Green, Cardinal. This is one of our most popular suits, and will give the best of satisfaction. Can usually be worn two seasons. The Interscholastic Shirt, any style; The Interscholastic Pants, any style; The Interscholastic Wool Stockings, No. 2R; The Interscholastic Quality Cap, any style; The Interscholastic Web Belt.

The Interscholastic Uniform, complete, $9.65

Net price to clubs ordering **$8.00** Detachable sleeves, 25 for **Entire Team**...Per suit cents each shirt, extra. No extra charge for lettering shirts with name of club.

The Pittsburg Club has adopted the idea of wearing a collarless jersey with striped sleeves under the flannel shirt, the sleeves of which extend only to the elbow, displaying the striped jersey underneath, and matching the striped stockings.

18

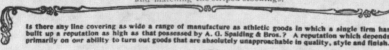

Baseball Uniforms for sale in the A.G. Spalding & Brothers 1904 Spring/ Summer Catalog. A complete Spalding uniform could be purchased for $15.60.

Flannel - The material of choice from the inception of bib fronts until knits replaced them during the early 1970s. Early flannels tend to be thick and heavy, much like a horse blanket. Later flannels are similar to the casual plaid flannel shirts worn today.

Grading

Fair/Poor - Numerous holes and large tears, heavy concentrated spotting, labels gone. Sections of jersey missing from moths or chemicals. Emblems gone. Major portions of jersey have heavy staining.

Good - Heavy wear, numerous repairs, labels gone or worn out. Scattered spotting and staining throughout. Emblems intact but worn, pulling away from jersey. Numerous thin spots.

Very Good - Medium wear, thin spots only on shoulder area. Labels intact and readable. Emblems intact. A few minor repairs, small holes or tears that do not detract from appearance. Minor spotting or staining throughout.

Excellent - Medium to light wear. No thinning in shoulders. Labels intact and easily readable. Emblems intact with no stretching or pulling away. No holes but minor repairs acceptable. Some discoloration but no concentrated stains.

Near Mint - Little wear, no thinning at all. All labels and emblems perfect with no matting of the material. No holes or repairs of any kind. Some discoloration or toning but no stains.

Mint - A like new jersey. Everything is perfect. Never worn.

Price Guide

Prices listed are for store-bought jerseys worn by any organized teams, i.e., town teams; industrial teams, etc.; famous colleges; Triple A leagues such as the Pacific Coast League or International League, etc. Famous barnstorming teams such as the House of David, Bustin Babe's, etc., would be worth much more than the prices listed. In addition, many of the patches, such as the 1939 Centennial or the 1951 American and National League patches, could be worth much more than the uniform it's sewn to.

For mint bib or laced front jerseys add 50%. All others, add 20-30%.

Child uniforms deduct at least 50% from given prices.

Boxed:
Bibs or lace fronts - add 30%
Others - add 10-20%
Tags - add 10-20%

As usual, any boxes or tags picturing famous players would be worth much more.

Prices listed are for pinstripes, whites and grays. Unusual colors such as forest green, bright red, etc., will command a premium of at least 10-20% of listed prices. Also, any really unusual or brilliant patches would increase desirability and hence, may add some value.

STYLE	V.G.	EXC.	NR/MT	SUPPLY
Bib front	$800	$1500	$2000	rare
Lace-up	$350	$750	$1000	rare
Shirt collar	$150	$300	$450	common
Cadet collar	$100	$200	$300	common
Sun collar	$75	$125	$200	common
Scoop collar	$50	$75	$100	common

In addition to the shirts or jerseys, baseball players also wore caps, belts, and pants, as well as socks and underwear. Early caps, belts, and pants have become very collectible. Early caps again are patterned after naval or military styles progressing in the 1870s to flamboyant styles and colors, some resembling jockeys, others a sport cap. Often seen with bold stripes or a star on top. Others had an outside headband or evolved into what has become known as the pillbox cap, then called the Chicago style if it had stripes, and the College style if it didn't. The Boston style is a rounded cap with a small bill, the Brooklyn, University, and Philadelphia style had short bills but higher profiles. It may prove to be a difficult task in determining whether or not you may own a very early baseball cap. Watch for large stars on top of early floppy hats and sporting goods retailer patches–this will help. Grading caps and pants will fall under the same guidelines as jerseys. Deductions for child sizes and other legends are identical for all parts of the uniform.

Cap Pricing

STYLE	V.G.	EXC.	NR/MT	SUPPLY
(watch for labels*).	$600	$1000	$1500	rare
Stars on top	$700	$1300	$1800	rare
Pillbox(Chicago style)	$400	$800	$1200	rare
Small bill (various)	$75	$125	$200	common
Standard flannel caps	$15	$25	$40	common

*Any documented baseball cap ca. 1850-80, if not listed separately

Belts and baseball pants are also collected to some degree. Trousers worn with the bib front jerseys might be hard to discern from any other trousers, but quilted baseball pants are easily spotted. They may be found quilted from waist to knee or just below the knee. Standard flannel pants command little collector interest and were worn throughout this century and before, while the quilted pants span a much shorter period, dating to the turn of the century. Belts, worn from the inception, are another item that really has only one collectible model, and that is the elastic and leather sporting belts worn from the 1860s until the turn of the century. The most collected style is the double buckle cotton web variety popular from the 1860s until the first decade of this century. Early teams, and sometimes the captain, would have their name imprinted on the

Pill box cap ca. 1890-1905.

Pill box cap ca. 1890-1905.

Pill box cap ca. 1890-1910.

Small bill cap ca. 1890-1905.

Early (ca. 1890-1910) small bill baseball cap.

belt making them extremely collectible. Plain leather belts, while hard to discern any particular time period, also are not eagerly sought. Early high-top baseball shoes, while an important piece of equipment, have not changed much except in height and are not highly collectible, but are listed since they often round out a display.

Other articles worn by players include sliding pads, popular by the early teens, and socks. Socks, aside from finishing off a uniform, are not collectible. Pads, on the other hand, if found endorsed by a famous player, have some value.

Miscellaneous Prices

ITEM	V.G.	EXC.	NR/MT	SUPPLY
Quilted pants	$125	$250	$375	rare
Flannel pants	$10	$20	$30	common

Spalding quilted baseball pants ca. 1890-1910.

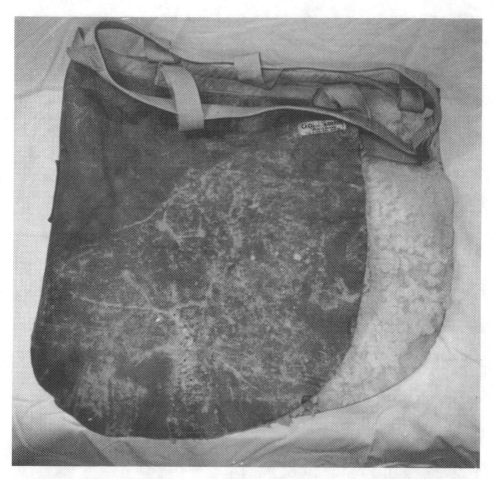

Leather and lambs wool sliding pads ca. 1900-20.

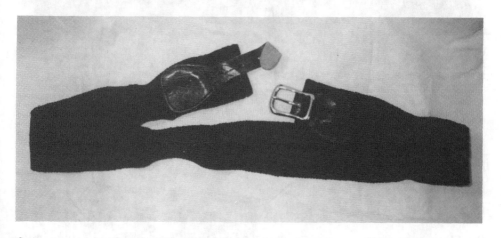

Canvas and leather baseball belt with single buckle ca. 1890-1920.

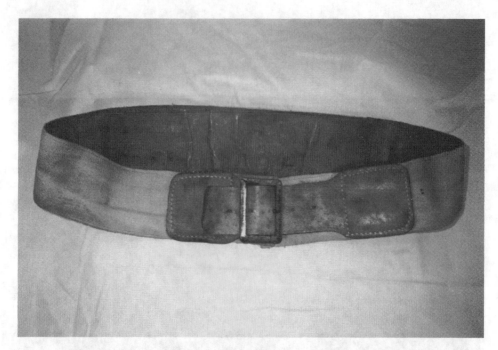

Spalding canvas and leather baseball belt with single buckle ca. 1890-1920.

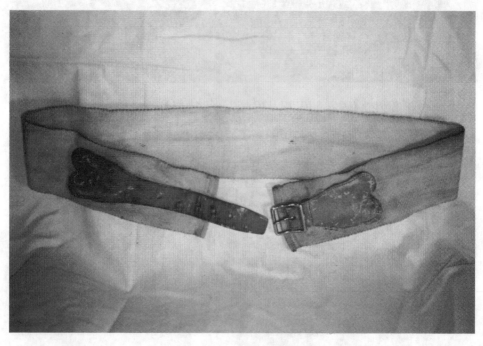

Spalding canvas and leather baseball belt with single buckle ca. 1890-1920.

Pair of early (ca. 1910) Spalding metal spike baseball shoes. Notice wingtip style toes.

Double buckle cotton canvas sporting belts

Marked captain	$300	$600	$900	rare
Team marked	$300	$600	$900	rare
Plain	$100	$150	$200	common
High top shoes	$50	$75	$125	common

Sliding pads Endorsed

Hofers	$50	$100	$150	varies
Stars	$40	$80	$120	varies
Plain	$10	$20	$30	common

Socks	$5-25

WILSON MADE TO MEASURE
BASEBALL UNIFORMS

Wilson Tailored Baseball Uniforms have been adopted and are worn by leading professional clubs in all leagues.

Each Uniform is made in exact accordance with the measurements of the individual player and is guaranteed to fit.

Stoutest materials of the finest quality—rugged, tough, uniform flannels especially woven and constructed to stand the severest wear—reinforced at all points where the greatest strain occurs.

Only perfect uniforms leave the Wilson shops—uniforms that are representative of all that is fine in workmanship, style, fit and durability of construction.

GRADE OO—MAJOR LEAGUE UNIFORM, COMPLETE $27.00
As Supplied to the National and American League Clubs

Made from the finest quality pre-shrunk 8-oz. wool Athletic Flannel, by experienced uniform tailors who know the requirements of the Big League players and who have put into this garment every practical feature to produce a uniform of style, comfort and durability. Shirt, Pants and Cap made of the same material.

GRADE O—MAJOR LEAGUE UNIFORM, COMPLETE $25.00

Same as OO—except that the shirt is a trifle lighter in weight—particularly desired in warmer climates.

GRADE AA—AMERICAN LEAGUE UNIFORM, COMPLETE $22.50

Made from the finest quality pre-shrunk 6-oz. wool Athletic Flannel, Shirt, Pants and Cap made of the same material. Workmanship, fit and general appearance equal in every respect to our best grade.

GRADE 1—UNIVERSITY LEAGUE UNIFORM, COMPLETE $19.00

Made from a fine quality pre-shrunk 6-oz. Athletic Flannel, especially constructed for strength and durability. Shirt, Pants and Cap made of same material.

GRADE 2—LEGION UNIFORM, COMPLETE $17.00

Made from a 6-oz. sturdy Athletic Flannel which can be depended upon to withstand the grueling treatment a player usually has in store for a uniform of this grade. Shirt, Pants and Cap made of the same material.

GRADE 3—HIGH SCHOOL UNIFORM, COMPLETE $15.00

Made from a heavy weight fine quality Athletic Uniform Flannel. Shirt, Pants and Cap of same material.

GRADE A3½—REGULATION UNIFORM
COMPLETE $13.50

Made of a new improved sturdy heavy weight Athletic Uniform Flannel embodying every necessary feature as regards strength, durability and patterns. A most satisfactory uniform at a low price. Shirt, Pants and Cap made of the same material.

GRADE 4—CHALLENGE UNIFORM
COMPLETE $11.50

Made from an improved, reliable Athletic Flannel which can be depended upon for service and equal in appearance to suits of better grades. Made in the same careful manner as all our uniforms. Shirt, Pants and Cap made of the same material.

GRADE 5—DEFIANCE UNIFORM
COMPLETE $9.50

This uniform is especially constructed for endurance and can be depended upon for good substantial wear. A well-made suit of fine appearance. Shirt, Pants and Cap of the same material.

GRADE 6—KNOCK-A-BOUT UNIFORM
COMPLETE $8.00

Our least expensive as well as our best are made in the same careful manner. Shirt, Pants and Cap of same material.

Write for Special Baseball Uniform Catalog, Showing Quality, Patterns and Full Details.

32

Ad taken from the Wilson Athletic Equipment 1932 Spring & Summer Catalog. Note the choices of uniforms (Major League, American League, University League, etc.) available to buyers.

FOOTBALL EQUIPMENT

Helmets
Other Epuipment:
    Noseguards
    Jerseys/Vests
    Shoulder Pads
    Shinguards
    Pants
    Shoes

Nice football display from California dealer.

HELMETS

The football helmet, in some form, has been around since before the turn of the century. An 1899 Horace Partridge & Company catalog listed the Victor and the Spalding Head Harness, both of which only have straps of leather going front to back and across with protection for the ears and little else. The rest of the head is exposed including your hair. The Victor Improved helmet covered the entire head in leather, with heavy felt on the inside. The Partridge Improved helmet went a step further by adding a sun bill like a baseball cap. The football head bandage was little more than an elastic headband made to protect the ears.

From these early beginnings, the football helmet, as we know it today, has drastically evolved. If you think that the only place you might find these old helmets is in the Football Hall of Fame in Canton, Ohio, you may be surprised. Much of the old football equipment used during the early days predating the National Football League's formation in 1922 is still out there. While there may be dozens of minor design differences and a rainbow of colors and makers, most helmets, as to collector value, will fall into a certain category and range. In addition to helmets, you will find identification and pricing for other accessories such as shinguards, rubber nose guards, trousers, shoes, shoulder pads, and jerseys.

Glossary

Helmet - Any item made for covering the head of a football player, regardless of style.

Aviator style - A style that is all-leather without any stiff form. It resembles an early race driver's or airplane pilot's hat, hence the designation. Usually constructed with elastic bands connecting the various parts, such as the forehead or the back of the neck. The ear protection hangs loose over the ears. The padding is the same as the flat top, heavy felt. Popular from the turn of the century until the late teens.

Composition helmets - Any leather will be on the inside. All composition outer construction introduced into the NFL during the late 1940s.

Dog ear - Refers to the style of ear protection or shape on aviator, rain cap and flat-top helmets. They usually hang loose and come to a point at the base, much like the ears on a basset hound. Popular style from 1900-20.

Endorsement models - These can range from top-of-the-line models such as Wilson's coach series such as Pop Warner and Knute Rockne to sandlot models bearing a decal of Notre Dame coach Frank Leahy.

Early football jersey, high waist pants, strap helmet, and small bill college cap on half mannequin.

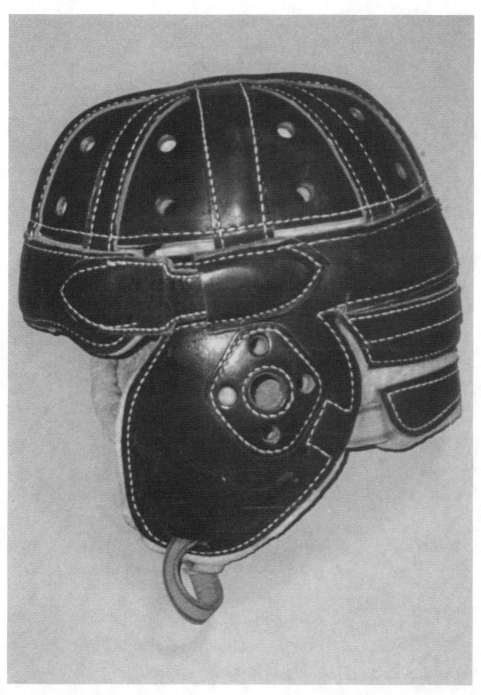

Unusual D & M metallic green all leather helmet with elastic construction ca. 1920s.

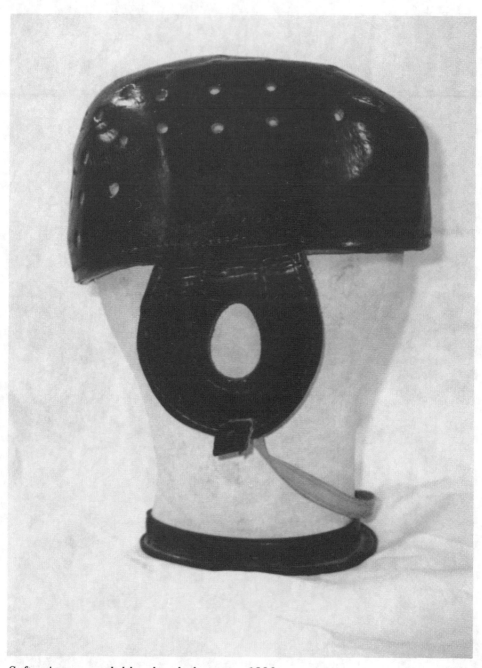

Soft raincap model leather helmet ca. 1890s.

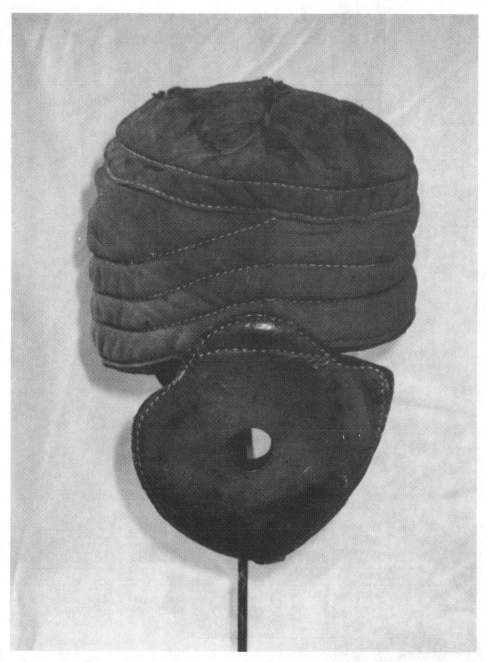

Canvas with leather ears flat top (unusually large dog ear style) ca. 1900-1920.

Leather dog ear with unusually high round crown ca. 1890-1910.

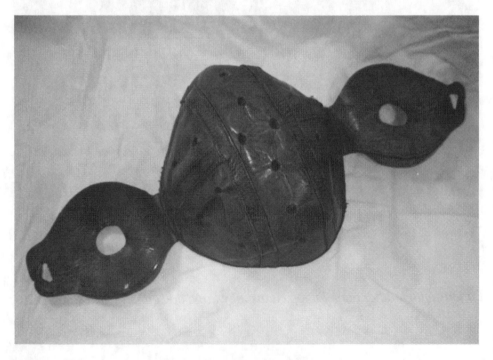

Top view of raincap style (early aviators) with dog ears.

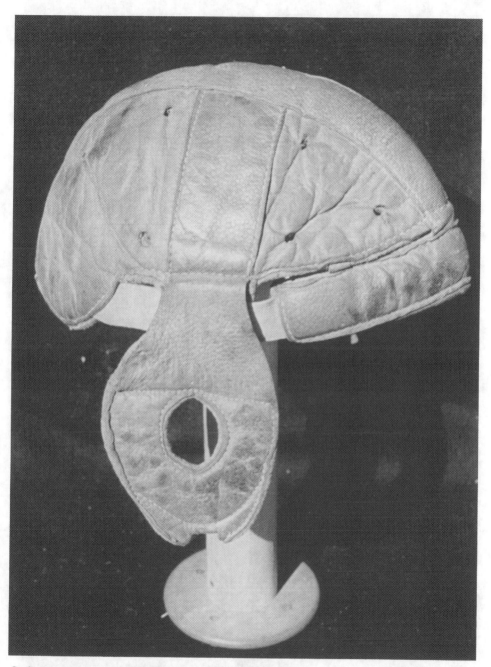

Soft dog ear model leather helmet ca. 1890-1910.

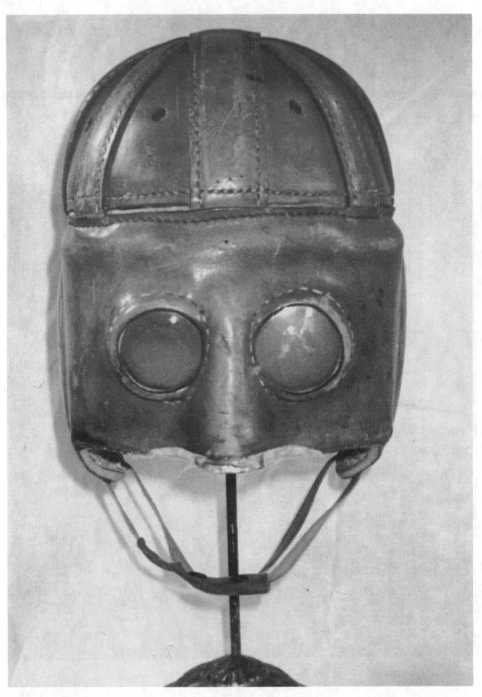

Executioner style helmet with sewn in face guard and glass added for eyes ca. 1920-30.

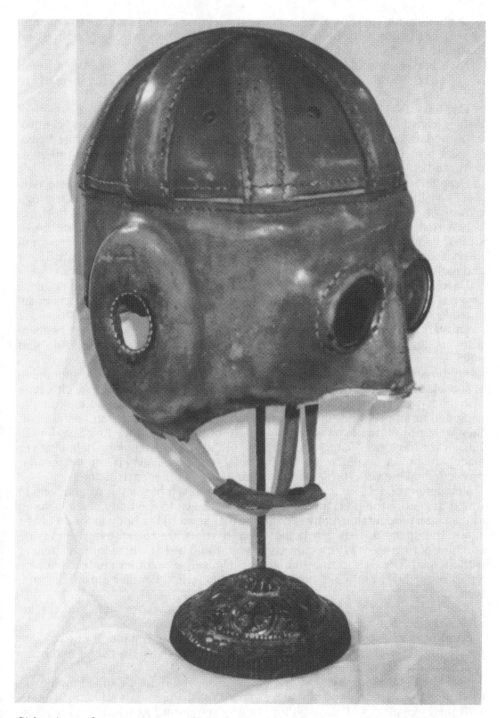

Side view of executioner style helmet with glass inserted in eye holes.

Executioner style - So called because the leather helmet extends to cover all or part of the face with holes for the eyes and nose. An extremely scarce and desirable item. Popular during the 1920s.

Face bar - A bar added to front of helmet for face protection. Often found bolted to old leather helmets and made standard equipment during the early to mid 1950s.

Flat top - A style of helmet denoted by its rather flat top. They were made of leather, canvas, or a combination of both. Popular from the turn of the century until the late 1920s. The usual padding in these helmets is an off-white heavy felt. Ear protection hangs loose from the body of the helmet, allowing them to be turned up and out of the way.

Grange style - All leather construction no longer made with the elastic pieces visible except, in some cases, the forehead piece. Has a rather high crown with contrasting straps of leather running both vertically and horizontally across the crown. Usual color is natural brown with black or dark brown straps. Padding will be a combination of canvas or leather crown straps and heavy felt or leather side construction. Popular during the mid to late 1920s and early 1930s. Most 1920s helmets have "Grange" style construction.

Hard shell - The crown of the helmet is a hard molded composition material covered with straps of leather. The side body is also leather. Padding is cushioned leather with strap suspension. Popular during the 1930s and 1940s.

Late all leather - Style popular until early 1950s. Heavy, all leather helmets with inside padding that resemble first all composition helmets. Wide and much larger than their earlier counterparts. A stiff helmet.

Pneumatic helmet - A rare style of helmet that had an inflatable donut made of soft black rubber on top and an air attachment with which to fill it. This type of helmet was supposed to soften a blow to the head. The donuts simply exploded on impact and had an active life of about one game, and as a result they were not on the market for any length of time. Introduced by Spalding in 1903, it was no longer listed by 1905. One of the strangest looking helmets ever made. The profile is similar to a tall body flat top and hanging round bottom ear protection. Made with the same heavy felt lining as other early helmets.

Princeton model - All leather style of helmet resembles a flat top but one in which the entire top piece of leather has been sewn to the body of the helmet, as if an afterthought. It usually is connected or sewn to the body in four to eight spots, the space in between being open. If you were to remove the outside stitching of the top of a Princeton style, you would be left with a football helmet without a lid. The ears, rather than hanging loosely as in other models, become a part of the body of the helmet. Padding is heavy felt. Popular during the mid-teens and 1920s.

Rain cap - An early style of helmet predating the aviator style and similar except thinner leather, less padding, slightly more rounded.

Sandlot model - Resembles early leather helmets but made of cheap compressed material resembling cardboard. Often found in bright colors and bearing endorsements of famous players.

Soft shell - Like an aviator style but has form, could not be rolled up like an aviator as the leather is too stiff and shaped, yet the helmet is still constructed with the large pieces of elastic allowing fit to conform to each individual. Suspension is sometimes a crisscross pattern in the crown made of canvas and leather. The ear protection may resemble the dog ear style but often is rounded

Flat top model helmet ca. 1890-1920.

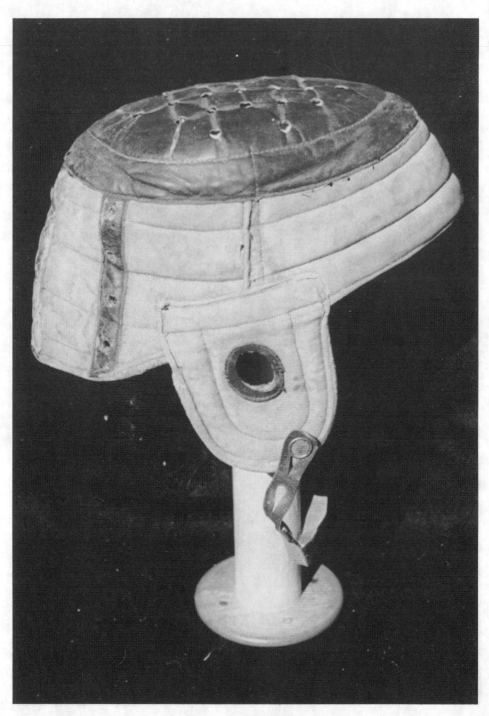

Canvas with leather top flat top helmet ca. 1890-1920.

All leather flat top helmet in its original box ca. 1910.

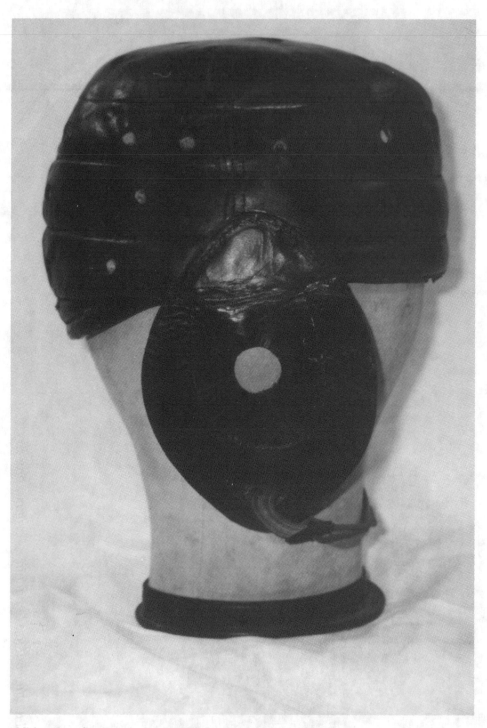

All leather flat top helmet with large ears ca. 1900-1920.

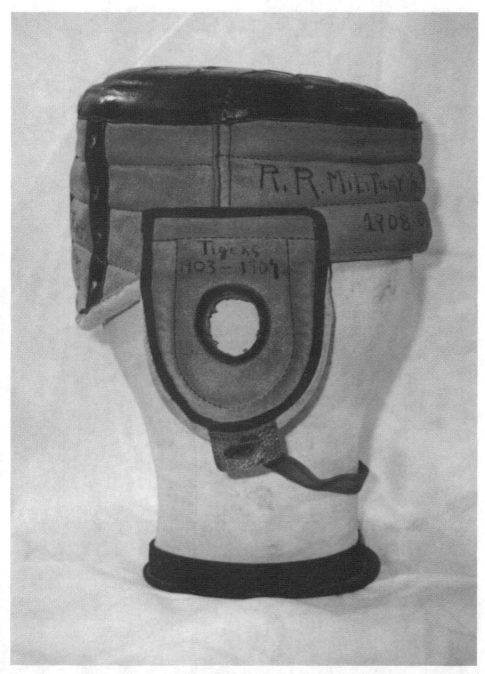

Canvas with leather flat top helmet with team writing on canvas ca. 1900-20.

All leather helmet ca. 1930.

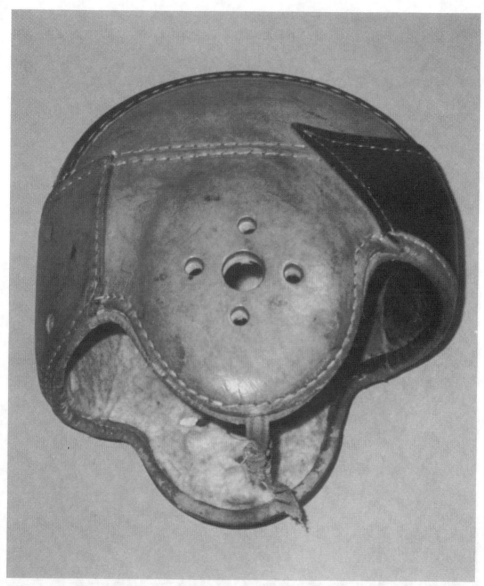

Side view of all leather ca. 1930s wing front football helmet.

Zuppke style leather helmet with elastic forehead piece ca. 1920s.

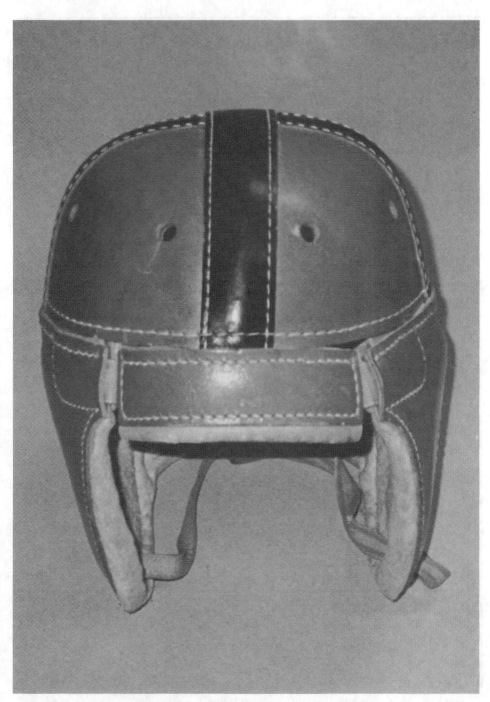

All leather helmet with elastic forehead piece ca. 1920-30.

Leather and hard shell helmet ca. 1930-40.

at the base instead of pointed. The biggest difference between this style and the aviator style is the lack of flexibility in a soft shell. Popular from late teens until early 1920s.

Stocking cap - The earliest form of football head apparel. This is nothing more than a cotton or wool knitted cap, sometimes with a tassel. Unless designated as such, it is tough to tell whether you have a stocking cap style. Watch for maker's stamps.

Strap helmet - A style made up of straps, all connecting at a central point on the top of the head. Made of leather or heavy canvas. Padding is felt and the ear protection hangs loose like the aviator and flat top. You can see a player's hair through a strap helmet. Popular from late nineteenth century until early 1920s.

(**Warning**: A similar helmet was used by hockey players in the 1940s through the 1960s. The chin straps on these will have snaps, not found on football helmets until after the demise of the strap helmet. Also the ears on the hockey version are open to allow the player to hear better. The football helmet will completely cover the ear with only minor holes for ventilation and hearing. Football chin straps will have a pull-through adjustment.)

Wing front - Refers to the piece of leather on the front of the helmet with pointed tips resembling wings. The same style adopted by the University of Michigan. Usually seen on hard shell helmets from the 1930s era and later.

Grading

Fair/Poor - Leather rotted and badly cracked, all the way through in places. Pieces missing with major holes and tears. Seams torn. Lining gone. Chin strap missing. Canvas torn, or writing evident, i.e., marker. Hard shell cracked or broken. Heavy aftermarket paint with major chipping. ("Aftermarket paint" means the helmet was painted privately, after leaving the factory.)

Good - Leather complete but dry with numerous cracks. Small holes in canvas. Minor writing visible, strap gone, lining loose. Small tears and seam repairs or loosening seams. Small cracks in hard shell. Scuffed with only traces of original color or repainted with cracks.

Very Good - Leather supple with minor cracking, no writing on outside except numbers. Strap gone. Lining intact. No holes but some seam loosening. No cracks in hard shell. Lots of outside scuffing and color loss, but all factory original.

Excellent - Leather supple with no cracking of surface. No writing. Strap intact. Lining intact. No holes or tears. Seams complete. Shell perfect. Minor outside scuffing. Factory original colors.

Near Mint - Leather perfect. Soft and supple. No cracking of surface. All lining perfect with no cracking. Strap intact. No tears, holes, or writing. Slight scuffing with all original and bright factory finish or color.

Mint - An unused helmet sans scuffing, writing, dirt, cracking, etc. Perfect inside and out with only shelf wear on high spots.

Leather and hard shell helmet ca. 1930-40.

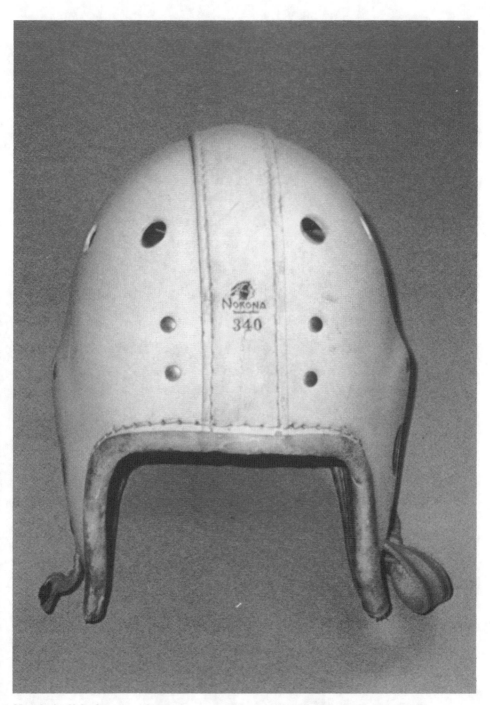

Hard shell helmet without face guard ca. late-1940s and early-1950s.

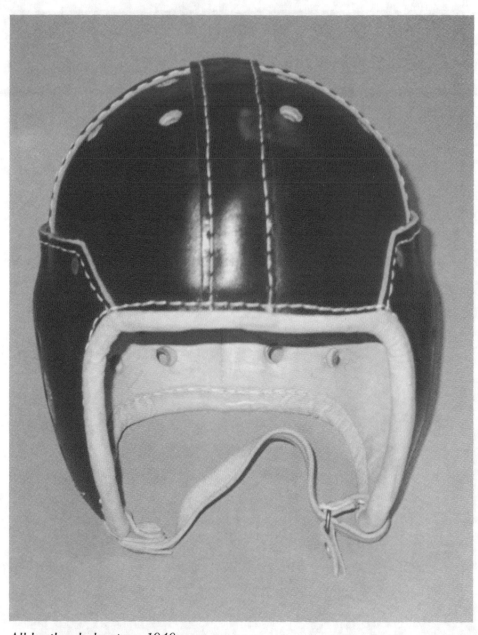

All leather helmet ca. 1940s.

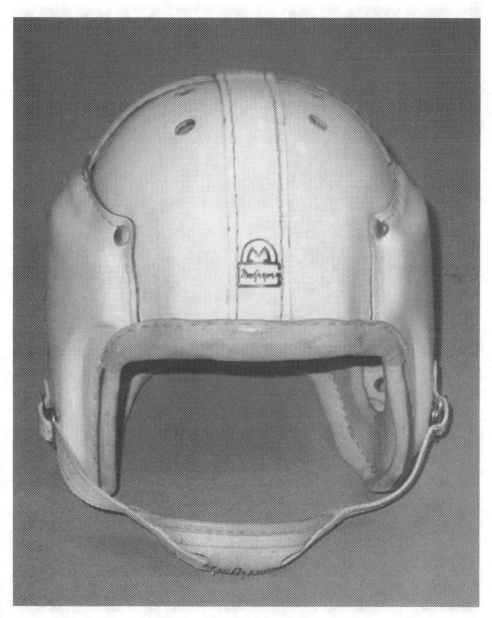

All leather high crown MacGregor ca. late 1940s.

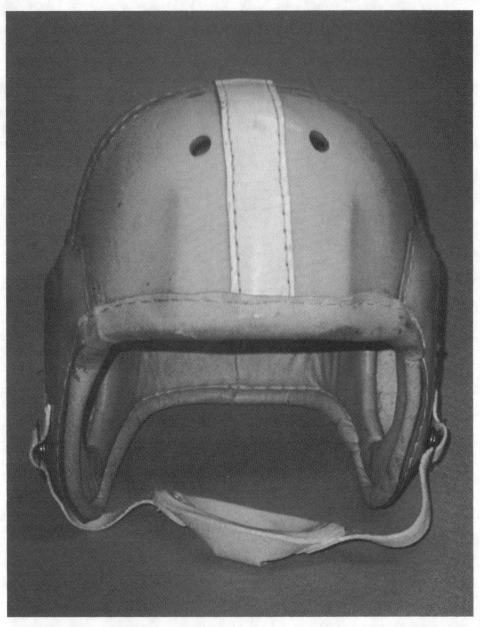

Front view of late-1940s early-1950s MacGregor pro style helmet from the last days of leather helmets.

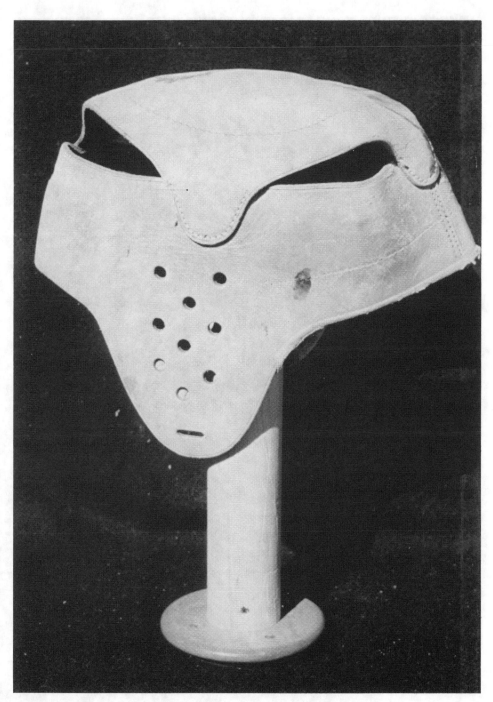

Early Princeton style leather helmet ca. 1890.

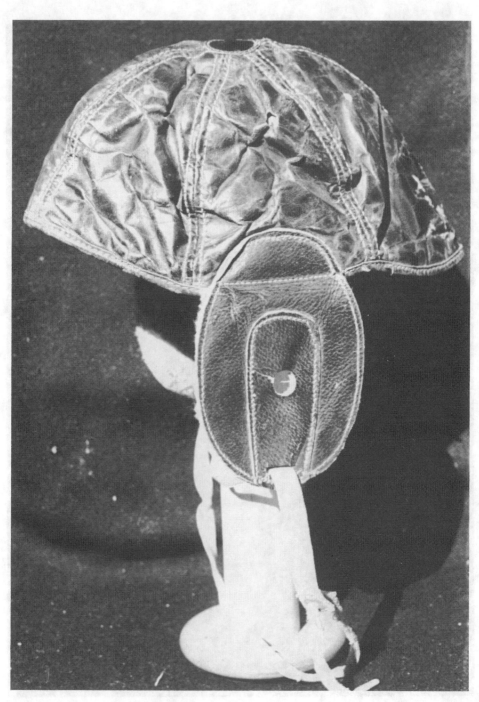

Early raincap helmet ca. 1890.

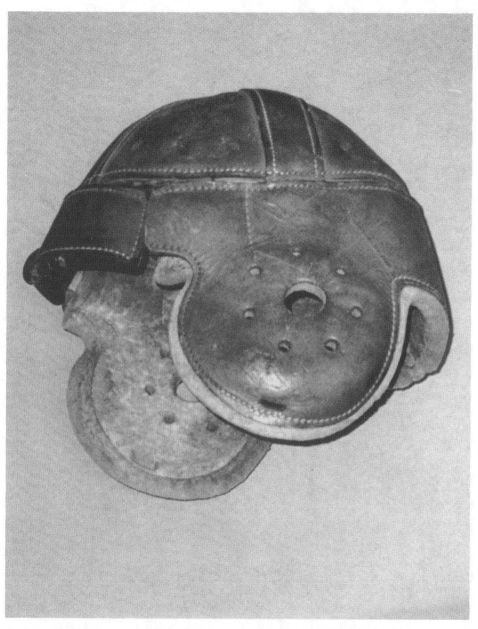

Soft leather helmet with elastic forehead piece ca. 1920s.

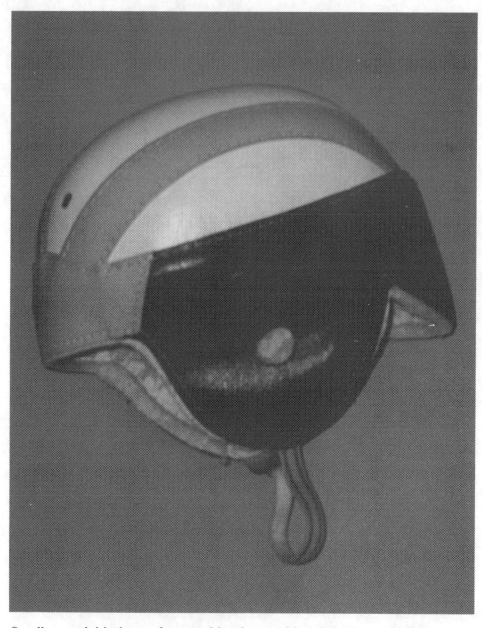

Sandlot model helmet of pressed leather and hard shell ca. 1940-50.

Canvas strap helmet ca. 1890-1915.

Impossible football stocking cap style dating to early 1880s. Watch for sporting goods labels. Verifiable examples would bring in excess of $800 but are extremely difficult to identify as football.

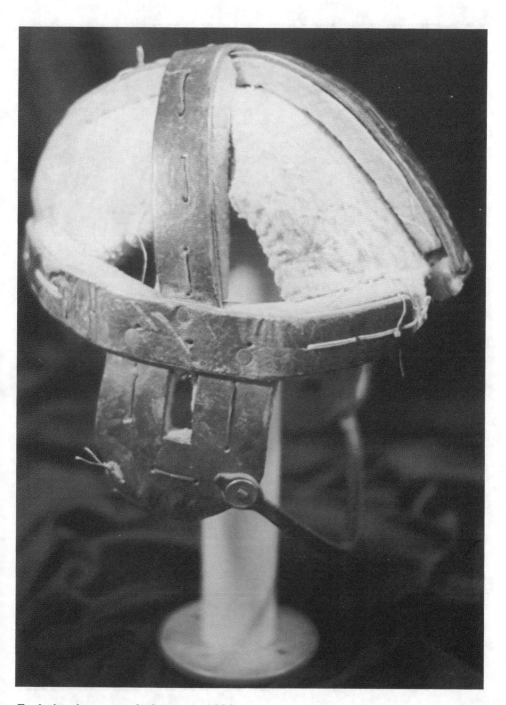

Early leather strap helmet ca. 1890.

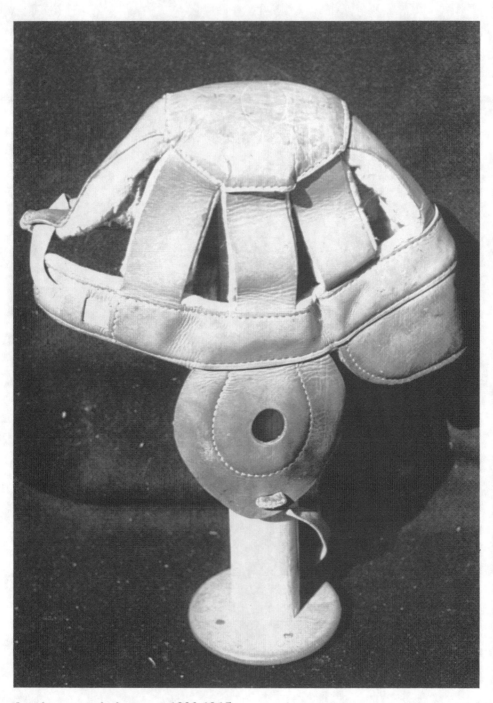

Leather strap helmet ca. 1890-1915.

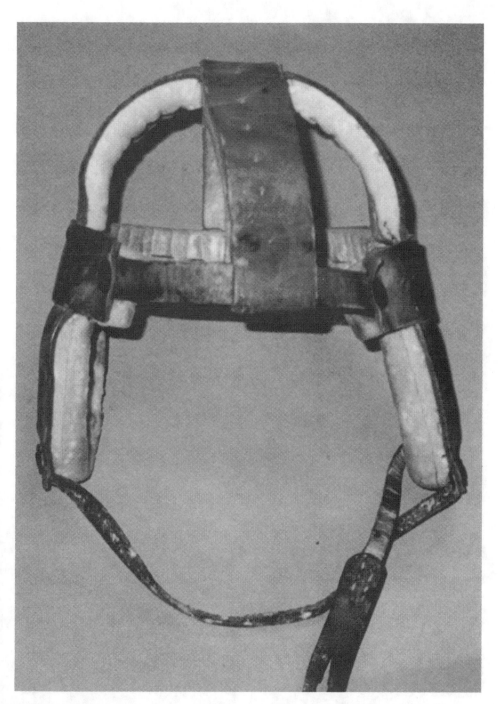

Early leather and felt strap helmet ca. 1890s.

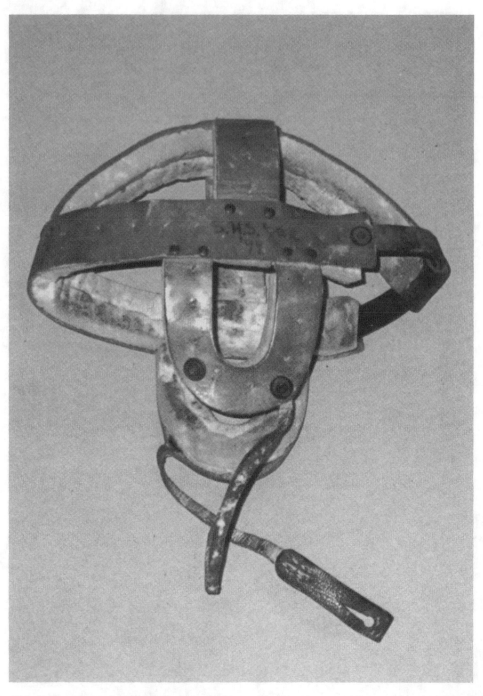

Side view of early leather strap helmet. Notice the metal grommets holding chin strap.

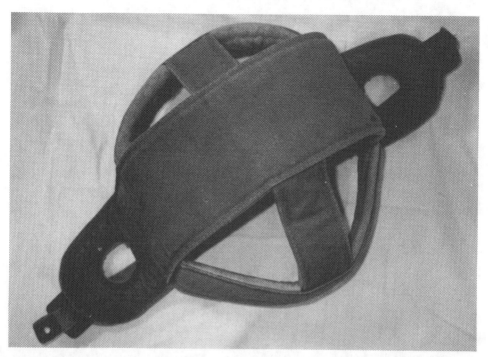

Top view of canvas strap football helmet.

Top view of leather strap helmet with deep Reach logo in crown, a super example.

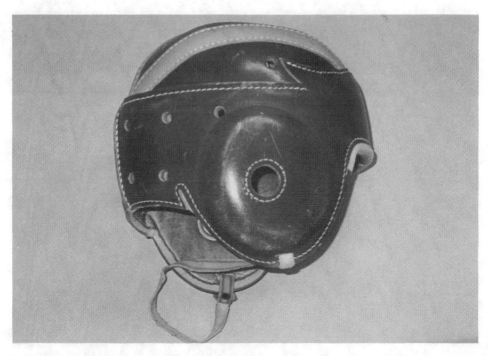

Side view of pristine wing-front leather helmet.

Michigan style wing front all leather helmet ca. 1930.

Wing front leather and hard shell helmet ca. 1930-40.

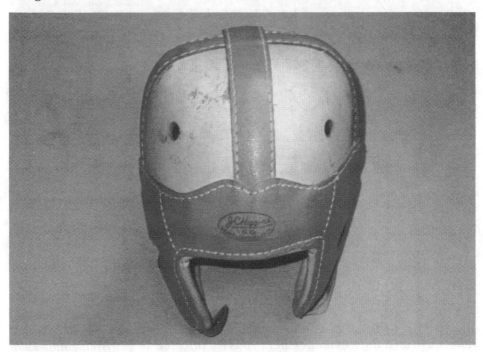

Leather and hard shell wing front helmet ca. 1930-40.

Wilson Intercollegiate Head Harness

68. Wilson Intercollegate Head Harness. Finest selected tan leather. Has thick layer of moulded soft sponge rubber in crown. (Patent applied for.) Moulded back extension completely covering the ears, lined with best quality white felt. Forehead piece has a soft leather sweat band and elastic adjustment. Crown and ear pieces perforated for ventilation. Overhead leather crown strips, with two extra reinforcing strips on front of crown. Crown and strips reinforced with fibre. The safest and best football helmet made. ....**Each, $10.00**

69. Wilson Intercollegiate head harness, made of selected black leather; otherwise same as 68 ....**Each, $10.00**

68 and 69

68 and 69
Showing Patented Sponge Rubber Feature Inside Crown

71. Wilson Head Harness. Finest selection firm black leather crown and back extension. Crown is lined with best quality white felt and in addition has a perforated soft sponge rubber pad. The back extension is moulded, completely covering the ears, white felt lined. The forehead piece has soft leather sweat band and elastic adjustment. Adjustable elastic chin strap with snap fasteners. Crown and ear pieces are perforated for ventilation. Overhead leather crown strips reinforced with fibre......**Each, $8.00**

72. Wilson Head Harness made of selected tan leather. Otherwise same as 71.
Each, $8.00

71 and 72

71 and 72
Showing Perforated Sponge Rubber Pad Feature inside crown.

70. Wilson Intercollegiate Head Harness. Finest selected black leather crown and moulded back extension. Equipped with the patented McGill chin piece which is made of firm leather, padded with felt and lined with soft leather which protects the chin. The back extension is moulded completely covering the ears. The forehead piece has soft leather sweat band and elastic adjustment. Lined throughout with the best quality of white felt. Crown and ear pieces are perforated, which allows perfect ventilation. Overhead leather crown strips re-inforced with fibre. **Each $9.00**

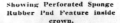

73

70

74. Wilson Head Harness. Popular model. Firm cream color strap leather crown and back extension. moulded leather ear pieces. Lined throughout with the best quality of pure white felt. Crown perforated for ventilation. The forehead piece has elastic adjustment with soft leather sweat band.
Each, $7.50

74

73. Wilson Head Harness. Harvard Model. Best quality firm black leather crown. Back and ear pieces of soft black leather. Lined with best quality white felt. Back and ear piece lined with soft yielding leather. Perforated for ventilation. Adjustable elastic chin strap with snap fastener. Overhead leather crown strips re-inforced with fibre. ....**Each, $7.50**

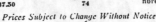

Prices Subject to Change Without Notice
6

Two pages from a 1925 Fall & Winter Wilson sporting goods catalog showing an array of available football helmets. Item 158 is what is now referred to as a flat top model. Item 76 is a Princeton style. (Notice the sewn-on top.) All of the others are variations of the elastic construction mid-1920s

Wilson Foot Ball Head Harness

82. Wilson Head Harness. Made of soft black leather padded with pure white felt and leather lined throughout. Perforated for ventilation. Adjustable chin strap........**Each, $6.00**

83. Wilson Head Harness. Made of firm black strap leather, lined throughout with heavy white felt. Soft leather sweat band, and elastic adjustment in forehead piece. Elastic chin strap. Perforated for ventilation.
Each, $5.00

84. Wilson Head Harness. Crown, back extension, and ear pieces, made of firm tan color strap leather, lined throughout with heavy white felt; soft leather sweat band and elastic adjustment in forehead piece. Elastic chin strap. Perforated for ventilation.
Each, $5.00

S3 and S4

76. Wilson Head Harness. Princeton model. Made of firm strap leather. moulded crown with pads at top; sides plain with pad at ears only. Soft leather sweat band; openings at crown and perforations at ears for ventilation ....**Each, $5.00**

78. Wilson Head Harness. Black leather crown, back extension and ear pieces. Lined with white felt throughout. Perforated for ventilation. Elastic adjustment in forehead piece. Elastic chin strap ....**Each, $3.50**

81. Wilson Head Harness made of black leather. Felt pad in crown and over ears. Balance unlined. Perforated for ventilation. Elastic chin strap ....**Each, $3.50**

78

77. Wilson Moulded Soft Sponge Rubber Helmet (Patent applied for). Stretches to conform to the shape of the head, light weight, well fitting and affords ample protection without binding. A helmet which will prove popular on account of its lightness, compactness and good feel....**Each, $3.00**

76 and 81

79. Soft black leather top and ear pieces felt lined, soft leather sweat band. Perforated for ventilation.
Each, $3.00

77

80. Tan imitation leather top and ear pieces, felt lined, soft leather sweat band. Perforated for ventilation.
Each, $2.50

79 and 80

Wilson All White Head Harness

157. Wilson All White Head Harness. Solid white leather crown and moulded back extension, completely covering the ears. The forehead piece has soft leather sweat band and elastic adjustment. Adjustable elastic chin strap with snap fastener. Lined throughout with the best quality pure white felt. Crown and ear pieces perforated to allow for ventilation.
Each, $8.50

158. Wilson All White Head Harness. Made of soft white leather, top and sides lined throughout with best quality pure white felt. Soft leather sweat band. Perforated for ventilation. ....**Each, $5.00**

157

15S

Prices Subject to Change Without Notice

7

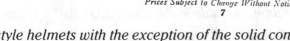

style helmets with the exception of the solid construction on item 82 and the all-rubber helmet, item 77. I have never seen nor heard of a rubber helmet like this existing and if one does surface, its price would be in the same range as an executioner model.

259

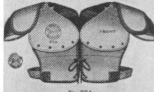

No. 88A

No. 282

FOOTBALL SHOULDER PADS AND HELMETS

In our line of football Shoulder Pads and Head Helmets we have made a careful selection of the best values offered by manufacturers of national reputation.

Our helmets and shoulder pads afford a maximum protection at a minimum price. All numbers in Helmets are colors complying with the football ruling on this subject.

Goldsmith Cantilever Shoulder Pad

No. 88A. Embodying the famous Cantilever construction. Attached to a foundation of white canvas and completely protecting the shoulders in heavy waterproof fibre covered with canvas arched over the shoulders so as to leave a space between the fibre and the body. This manner of construction distributes the weight of the blow over the entire pad. Moulded solid leather shoulder caps padded with white felt. Additional collar bone protection of moulded fibre. Wide elastic chest straps. Specified by the majority of colleges. Light in weight. Each........................$8.50

No. 32

Cantilever Lightweight Varsity Shoulder Pad

No. 32. This pad is without doubt the best value we have ever offered in a pad at this price. Kapok padded cantilever style with heavy gauge fibre over shoulders, chest and back. A great feature of this Kapok padding is that it will give full protection but will not add weight by absorbing moisture. Large fibre shoulder caps padded with white felt. Leather hinged fibre shoulder joint protectors. Elastic size straps insure a close body fit. Each....$5.50

No. MR

No. 167

Talbot Special Shoulder Pad

No. 167. A model that has proven its popularity the last few seasons. Made of tan strap leather with white felt padding. The pad is built to come down well over the chest and afford a most thorough protection. Light weight and practical. Each........................$5.00

Knox Interscholastic Model Shoulder Pad

No. 157. Made of sole leather with white felt padding. Moulded leather, felt lined shoulder caps and collar bone protectors. Leather extension over shoulder joints. Elastic shoulder bands. Adjustable lacing front and back. A splendid High School number. Each........................$4.50

No. 197H

No. 137

Standard Model Shoulder Pad

No. 1. A light weight pad, made of fine quality white felt, with special tanned strap leather; moulded fibre shoulder caps and collar bone protectors; round elastic under arms, laced front and back with "Rapid Lacer" in front. Each........................$3.50

Hanley-Bachman Aviator Model Helmet

No. 282. A light weight helmet designed primarily for the backfield men, although in some instances coaches have specified this model for the entire team. It cannot be jarred over the eyes and is so designed that it will not obstruct the player's vision from any angle. Black grain leather moulded crown over moulded fibre with a layer of foam rubber between crown and the felt padding. Leather lined throughout. Moulded fibre ears with some type of padding as in crown. Elastic chin strap. Comes in sizes, so be sure to specify sizes in ordering. Each........................$9.00

No. 184H

No. 2

Mercury Model Helmet

No. MR. A lineman's helmet that affords the most protection we have ever seen in a helmet. One piece moulded leather crown and one piece moulded fibre crown backing with white felt padding. Canvas web suspension straps in crown. One piece moulded fibre ear pieces with felt lining covered with soft, white leather. Elastic straps in back of helmet which holds it snugly to head and base of skull. Black leather with tan "Mercury" wing trim. Sizes Small, Medium or Large. Each........................$7.50

Reach Varsity Helmet

No. 197H. Tan crown with black forehead piece and tan cross strap. Rethreaded moulded fibre crown. White felt lining throughout, with leather lined sweat band. Inner web suspension crown. Elastic through the back to hold snugly to base of skull. Well ventilated moulded fibre ear pieces. Elastic chin strap. A splendid number for the entire team. Sizes, Small, Medium or Large. Each........................$6.50

Neill Intercollegiate Special Helmet

No. 184H. Dark brown leather moulded crown stiffened with fibre and reinforced with light tan cross straps. Extends well down in back protecting base of skull. Inner web suspension crown. White felt lining throughout with leather lining in sweat band. Moulded fibre ear pieces. Elastic forehead adjustment and elastic head strap. For a moderately priced helmet you can't go wrong on this one. Each........................$5.00

No. 79T

Elliott Full Protection Standard Model Helmet

No. 79T. Ventilated tan crown with black leather cross straps. Crown reinforced with fibre. Canvas inner web suspension crown. White felt lining ear pieces and back. Leather lined elastic adjustable forehead piece. Elastic chin strap. A good standard high school number and one that, as its name implies, affords ample protection. Each........................$4.00

Painting Your Football Helmets

Some of the Schools and Colleges want their football helmets to be their school color or some color other than the usual standard colors of the store helmets. A small can of "Duco" or any good Lacquer in the desired color can be obtained from your nearest paint dealer. It will dry over night. Apply with regular paint brush.

Showing inner web suspension crown. A feature of all of our helmets with the exception of the No. 282.

Football shoulder pads and helmets for sale in the Elliott 1931 Fall & Winter Sports Catalog No. 56.

Spalding's Pneumatic Head Harness
PATENTED

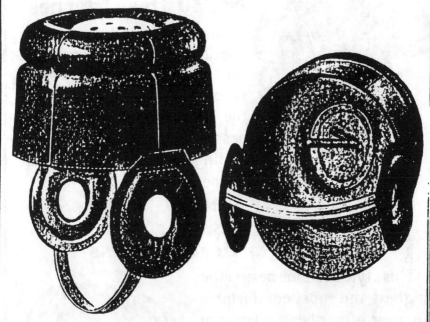

This represents really one of the greatest improvements that has so far been invented in the way of equipment for foot ball. It is made of soft black leather with an inflated crown. The pneumatic part of the head harness is sufficient to give ample protection with space left for ventilation through heavy wool felt. In every particular it is made in accordance with the official rules. Heartily endorsed by prominent players and trainers who have examined it thoroughly. When ordering specify size of hat worn.

No. 70. Each, $5.00

A. G. SPALDING & BROS.

Page from a 1905 Spalding Fall/Winter catalog featuring the ultra rare pneumatic helmet.

Spalding's Improved No. 50 Head Harness

Heavy sole leather crown; ventilated and with improved ear pads; used with great success last year, and one of the most popular head harnesses made. Used by the leading colleges throughout the country.

No. 50.   Each, $4.00

Spalding's Head Harness

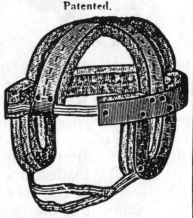

Patented.

This style head harness is the highest and most comfortable to wear of any head guard yet devised. It is made of tan leather and thoroughly padded with wool felt half an inch thick, with an elastic to go under the chin, and is adjustable to any size head. It is a thorough protection to the crown and back of the head, also to the ears.

No. 35.   Each, $2.50

A. G. SPALDING & BROS.

NEW YORK   **CHICAGO**   **DENVER**

Two pages from an 1899 Spalding Fall/Winter catalog. The earliest dog ear style (item 50) and two early open or strap helmets as they are not referred to.

Spalding's
Head Harness No. 30

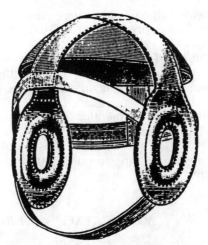

Designed by H. B. Conibear, trainer, University of Chicago. The crown piece is made of oak tanned leather molded to shape. The ear pieces are well padded, and the harness complete gives ample protection to all parts. A very light harness, yet amply strong.

No. 30.   Each, $3.00

Handsomely illustrated catalogue sent free to any address.

A. G. SPALDING & BROS.

NEW YORK   CHICAGO   DENVER

Price Guide

Boxed add:
Flat tops, straps, aviators - add at least 50%
Other leather models - 20-40%
Composition - 10-20%

If a box pictures a player, value would be much more.
Tags would add about 20% to prewar models, 10% postwar.

All prices are for adult size 7 or larger. Smaller sizes deduct 20% on any flat top, aviator, Princeton, or strap helmet; 30% on any other outside leather helmet; 50% on composition. No deductions on executioner styles.

Stunning factory colors such as metallic green or bright yellow, etc., are extremely desirable and would add a premium to any helmet.

Values for stocking caps would range around $800 and up, but would have to be examined individually.

TYPE	V.G.	EXC.	NR/MT	SUPPLY
Aviator/Rain cap	$175	$350	$500	common
Compo, no face bar	$25	$50	$75	common
Compo w/Hofers	$50	$75	$150	varies
Compo w/stars	$35	$60	$125	varies
Plastic w/player endorsement $10-35 common				

Leather or hard shell helmets with Hall of Fame, major college or famous coaches

	V.G.	EXC.	NR/MT	SUPPLY
coaches	$150	$300	$450	varies

(An early Red Grange or Bronco Nagurski would add at least 50%)

TYPE	V.G.	EXC.	NR/MT	SUPPLY
Other endorsements	$100	$200	$300	varies
Executioner	$400	$800	$1200	rare
Flat top	$250	$450	$650	common
Grange style	$125	$200	$350	common
Hard shell	$75	$150	$250	common
Late all leather	$75	$150	$250	common

Pneumatic (in grading a pneumatic, the inflatable donut must hold air to be
exc.) $400 $800 $1200   rare

Princeton $250 $450 $650   rare

Sandlot leather $25 $50 $75   common
Above w/player endorsements, add 10-20% varies

Soft shell $125 $200 $350   common

Strap $200 $400 $600   common
Above prices for canvas or leather & canvas. All leather, add 10%

OTHER
EQUIPMENT

Rubber noseguards, 1890-mid-1920s. Hard rubber with elastic strap that went around the head. Covered nose and mouth. Made with or without removable mouthpieces. Some seen with 1891 patent dates.

Conditions: very good (minor cracks or chipping, elastic replaced); excellent (no cracks but some edge chipping, original elastic); near-mint (no cracking or chipping, original elastic).

Add 20% for noseguards with removable mouthpieces.

Add 30% for original box.

Noseguard	$100	$200	$300	common

Jerseys - Early jerseys such as the worsted football striped sweaters and vests are extremely rare. Look for sporting goods labels to be sure it's football and not just an old sweater. Jerseys with the sure grip vertical stripes, the snap crotch, and made of worsted yarn are also desirable. Others lack the vertical attached stripes but may come in bright colors with stripes on the arms. Deciding whether or not you have a football jersey is tough–again watch for sports labels, i.e., Wilson, Spalding, D&M, etc.)

Early striped turtleneck worsted football jerseys dating from the turn of the century would sell in the $400-1000 range depending on condition (holes, etc.). They are extremely rare.

Early vests are also extremely rare and would sell in the $400-1000 range.

1920-30 style jerseys with the button crotch, of heavy wool and sporting sure grip cloth vertical stripes would sell in the $200-400 range.

1920-30 style jerseys without the vertical sure grip stripes would sell in the $100-300 range.

Any other pre-1950 jerseys would sell in the $50-200 range depending on colors, condition, thickness, etc.

Shoulder pads - Early shoulder and collar pads, ca. 1910, are nothing more than felt and leather, rather flat, which laid on the shoulders and strapped under the arm. Later pads were made of composition with heavy padding. Pads are sometimes found with player endorsements. They are not very collectible unless needed for a display. Prices for early flat pads run around $75-100 while hard pads sell in the $25-50 range. Hip pads, made of the same materials as the shoulder pads, are even less valuable–usually they are thrown in on the deal. If sold, they would probably be worth $5-10.

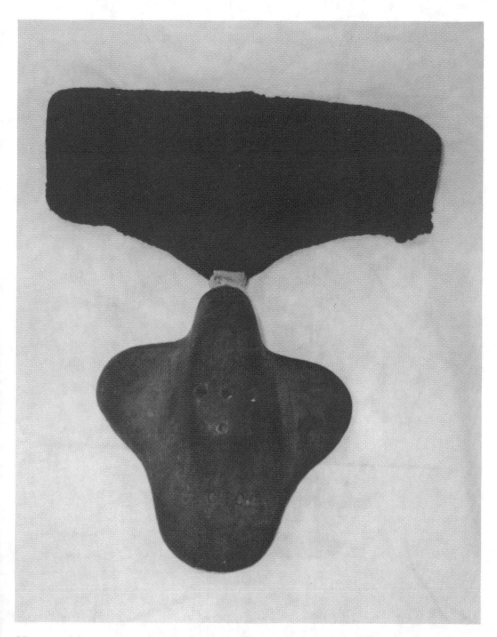

Victor rubber noseguard attached to original headband ca. 1890.

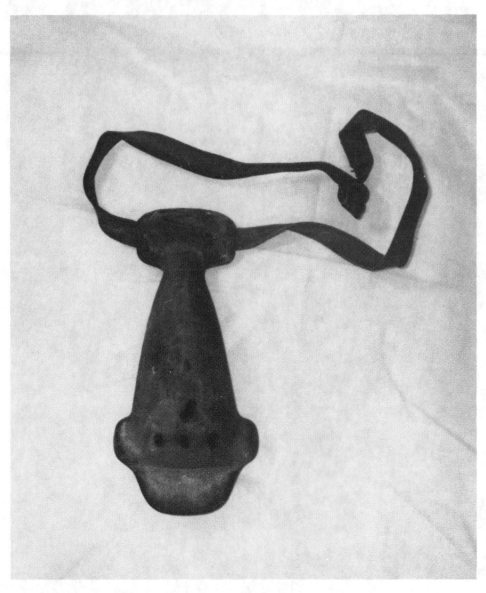

Standard style rubber noseguard ca. 1890-1920.

Front view of rubber football noseguard dating from 1890-1920. This one has the removable mouthpiece.

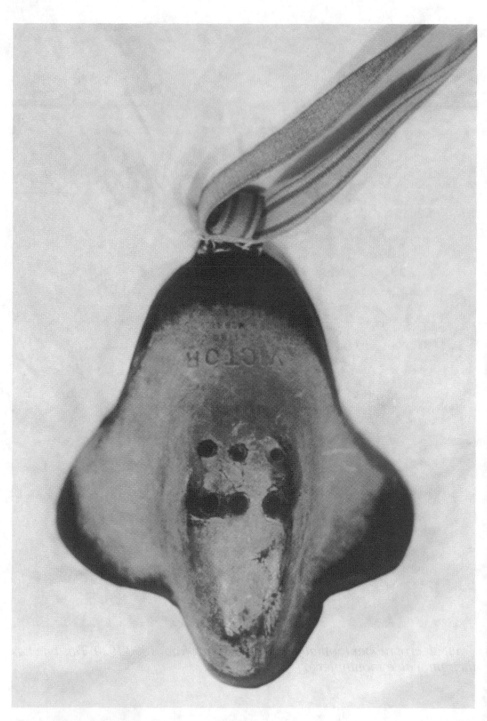

Front view of Victor sporting goods rubber football noseguard. Notice breathing holes and original elastic.

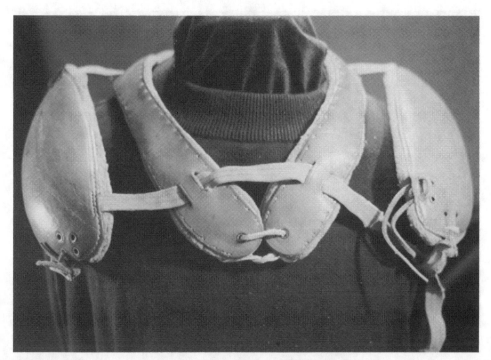

Early leather and canvas shoulder pads ca. 1900-20.

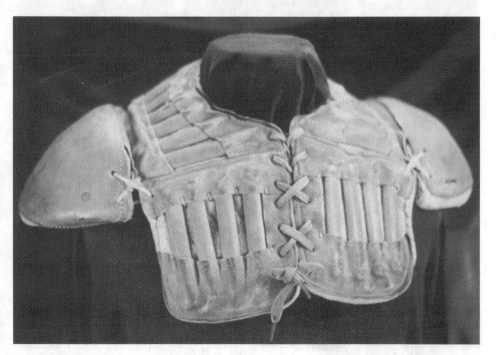

Early reed shoulder pads ca. 1900-1910.

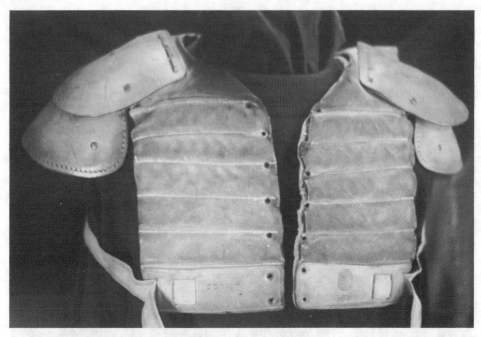

Shoulder pads with extended breast plate ca. 1920.

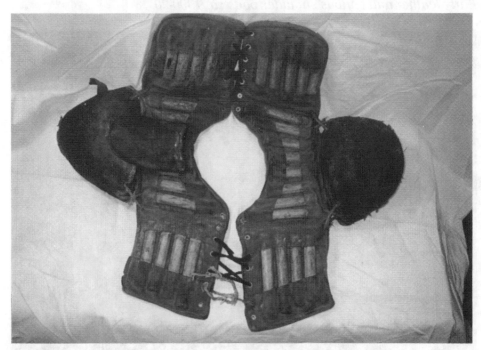

Ca. 1890 wood and bone reeded shoulder pads. Rare and unusual pads constructed of real bone, bamboo reeds, and leather.

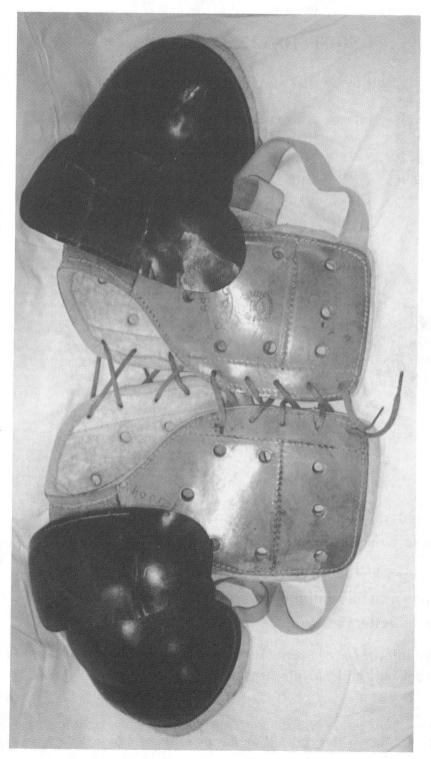

Front view of nice two-tone leather football shoulder pads ca. 1910-30.

FOOT BALL JERSEYS.

Full fashioned and finest in the market.

No. 1 P   Jersey, Roll collar, plain colors,   . $4 00
 "   1 PX   "   Striped collar, cuffs and skirt,   4 50
 "   1 PS   "   Horizontal stripes, any width,   5 00
 "   2 P   "   Cut Worsted, plain   colors,
                       roll collar, ...   2 50

In ordering send chest measure, sleeve from center of back to wrist, with elbow bent.

Name worked in on breast of Jersey, per letter,   . $0 50
Letters or name embroidered on Jersey, per letter   0 25
Flannel letters sewed on, per letter,   .   .   .   0 15

We offer a Lace Front Jersey with turned down collar, for foot ball and bicycle use, at $3.50 each.

Two pages from an 1899 Spalding Fall/Winter catalog featuring wool sweaters and hats. (You can tell by the illustrations why it would be a

Spalding's New Elastic Foot Ball Caps.

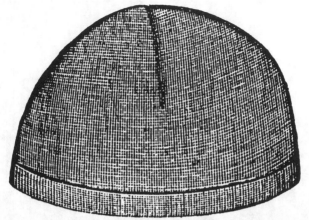

This new cap is designed for protection for the ears and hair. Made of woven silk and thread and very close fitting. Players suffering with sore ears, it is an absolute protection. Used for the first time last year by leading foot ball players. For use in match and practice games it is indispensable.

Price, each **$2 50**

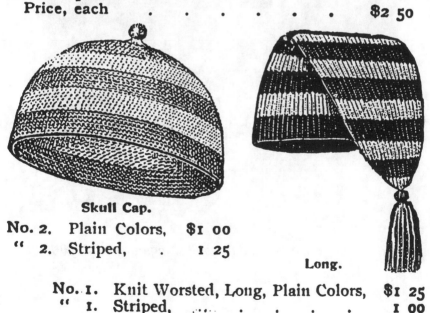

Skull Cap.

No. 2. Plain Colors, **$1 00**
" 2. Striped, . 1 25

Long.

No. 1. Knit Worsted, Long, Plain Colors, **$1 25**
" 1. Striped, ... 1 00

difficult task to determine whether or not a piece is sports related, if the tag is missing.)

Front view of canvas covered reed football shinguards ca. 1890-1910.

Quilted football pants (quilting all around unlike baseball quilts, which usually cover a portion of the pants) ca. 1900-20.

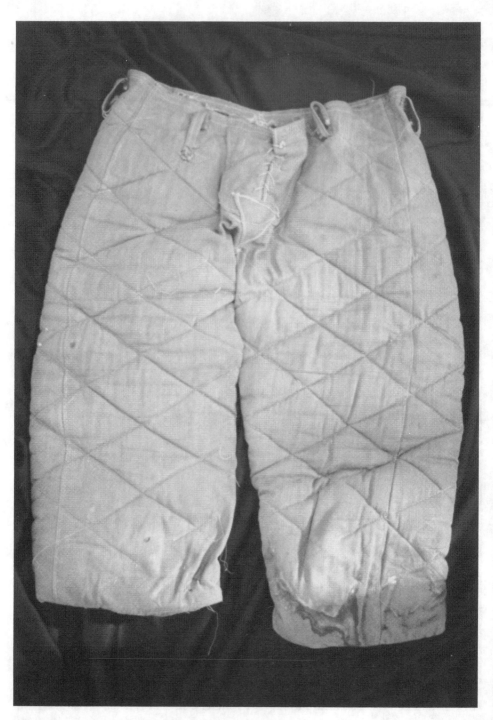

Diamond pattern moleskin pants ca. 1900-1920.

Reeded tops and quilted bottom football pants ca. 1900-1920.

Nice football display of early and rare football vest with reed pants and football shinguards along with other helmets, gloves, and awards.

Nice pair of Spalding football shoes with removable cleats ca. 1910-30.

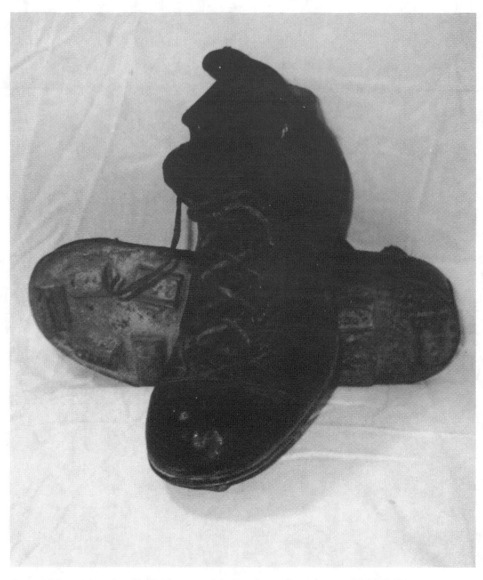

Pair of high-top football shoes with leather cleats ca. 1890-1910.

FOOTBALL PANTS—HOSE

Instructions for Ordering

Football Pants come only in even waist sizes. In measuring for pants give exact waist sizes but do not draw the tape line too tightly about the waist.

Elliott Varsity Model Combination Football Pants Outfit

No. 11BM7. This outfit consists of the No. 11 Shell Pants, the No. BM "Bo" McMillan Kidney Pads and one pair No. 7 Fibre Thigh Guards. Complete $14.75

Elliott Varsity Model Shell Pants Only

No. 11. Made of 8.60-ounce O. D. duck with kapoc knee pads sewed in and leather covered knees. Pockets for inserting Thigh Guards. Tunnel belt loops at back and regulation belt loops in front. Reinforced ventilated crotch. Knees are cut so that they will not slip up when wearer crouches. A light weight form-fitting shell pant that will fit perfectly over any kidney pads. Each $5.00

"Bo" McMillan Kidney Pads

No. BM. Designed for "Bo" McMillan, famous football coach of Kansas State College. It is light in weight, a perfect protector and an entirely new idea in construction. Have you ever noted the way that the sectional shell of a crawfish operates? Well, that is the way the hip and spine fibre works on this pad. There is absolutely no binding, no matter what position the player assumes. White felt padding with canvas covering. Elastic web straps in back will adjust this pad to fit any player. Web strap and buckle front. Each $7.50

One-Piece Molded Fibre Thigh Guards

No. 7. As the name implies these are one-piece, curved, moulded fibre thigh guards with felt around the edge. Designed to fit the thigh guard pockets of No. 11 pants or any other standard football pants. Per Pair $2.25

Elliott University Model Football Pants

No. 46. This model offers the best value in a high grade football pant possible to produce. Made of 8.60-ounce water repellent O. D. duck. Built in kapoc padded cantilever style hip and kidney pads with curved fibre on either side and leather reinforcement at bottom edge of fibre. Adjustable one-piece moulded thigh guards and fibre clipping guard. Kapoc knee pads and leather reinforcing patches on outside of pant at knees. Tunnel belt loops at the back and regulation front belt loops. Note the side view cut of this pant showing how pant conforms to the body when player is in crouching position. Each $11.75

Elliott Full Protection Model Football Pants

No. 5W. A pant made to our own specifications, with the thought uppermost of giving the High School player the same protection, style and fit accorded in higher priced pants. White felt lined canvas covered hip and kidney pads with fibre protection at sides. One-piece moulded fibre thigh guards. Well padded knees. A strong, durable, well-designed pant that will give wonderful service. Each $6.75

Elliott High School Special Football Pants

No. 4. This pant is also a popular choice with some of the High Schools. Made of good quality duck that will wear well. Gray felt canvas covered kidney pads, three-piece fibre thigh guards and padded knees. Leather strap and buckle on front with additional belt loops so that belt may also be used if desired, although belt is unnecessary with the front buckle feature. Each $5.00

Elliott Ward School Model Football Pants

No. 4B. The Ward School boy has arrived at the point where he wants a real football pant, not an imitation. The No. 4B football pant is made the same in all respects as the No. 4 excepting it is strictly a boy's pant. Suitable for boys from 10 to 14 years. No waist measure larger than 32 inches. In ordering give age and waist measure of the boys for whom pants are desired. Each $4.00

Elliott Leather Football Belts

No. 2. Made from the best black cowhide strap leather, 1¼ inches wide. Sizes 30 to 44. Each 50c

Football Hose

The cuts show three standard patterns in football hose. We carry in stock Style J in all standard solid colors. In ordering hose simply add the style letter to the number of the hose and give colors desired. In ordering two-color hose the first color mentioned is always the main color of the hose, the second being the stripe or lower color. We can furnish any special striping to order. Our regular stock hose are footless, but if you prefer hose with feet they can be furnished at no additional cost.

Hose Prices

No. H291. Good weight, ribbed, pure wool. In stock in Style J. Per pair....$1.35
No. H3. Heavy weight, pure wool, ribbed. To order, per pair.................1.50
No. H39H. An extra heavy weight, pure worsted. To order, per pair.........2.50
No. HC. Good weight, cotton ribbed. In stock in Style J. Per pair...........90c

Sanitary Hose

No. 90L. A special light weight, all white, full length hose, to wear with footless hose. Sizes 10, 11 or 12. Per pair.............................25c
No. 90S. These are the socks or half-hose, preferred by some for wear with the footless hose. Sizes 10, 11 or 12. Per pair.............................20c

Plain White, Short Length Hose

No. 21GS. These are a strong white cotton hose with 7½-inch finished tops. Sizes 9 to 12. Per pair.............................25c
No. VBS. Pure white bleached wool with 3-inch ribbed finish tops simply long enough to turn down over the tops of shoes. Sizes 9 to 12. Per pair...........50c

Sanitary Cotton Football Undershirts

No. 731S. This is a good quality white cotton shirt with full length sleeves, to be worn under jersey. Each 90c
No. 735S. A quarter sleeve shirt, same as above. Each 60c
No. 280. A sleeveless shirt, same as above. Each 50c

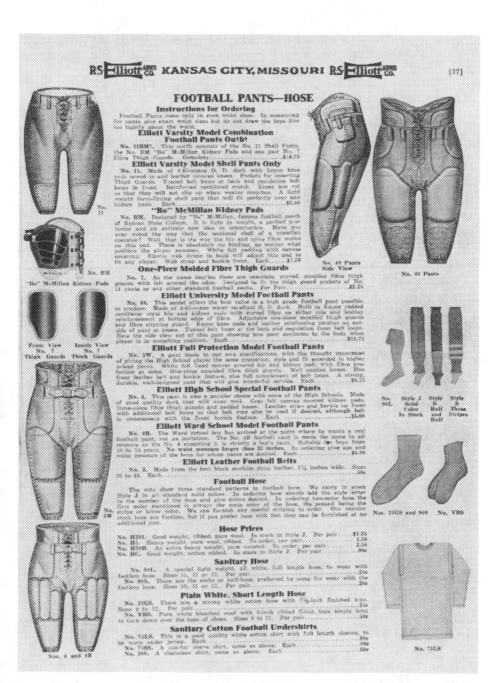

Miscellaneous football gear for sale in the Elliott 1931 Fall & Winter Sports Catalog No. 56.

Shinguards - Made of leather or canvas with wooden reeds and strapped to the shins. Popular from the turn of the century until the 1920s. They usually sell in the $75-125 range.

Pants - The most desirable of all football pants are the moleskin style from the turn of the century. They are a light brown, with lace-up front. They are usually padded with heavy curled hair at the hips and knees. Quilted canvas of the same time period would come next. Then come the early canvas models with the high waist and wooden reeds in the front. Other early high waist designs would follow. Plain late model canvas would not be worth much except to someone completing a uniform.

Moleskin pants	$200-500
Quilted canvas	$150-300
Reeded high waist	$75-150
Other high waist	$50-100
Common canvas	$25-50

Child sizes are not collectible unless moleskin, (deduct 30%).

Shoes - Mostly an afterthought to collectors unless they are high top shoes with wooden cleats. These sell in the $50-75 range.

Socks - See Miscellaneous Chapter.

BALL EQUIPMENT

Baseballs
Footballs
Basketballs

BALLS

Baseballs, footballs, and basketballs are items without which those games could not be played. But are they collectible? And if so, what is an old football worth and which ones are collectible? The variety of each makes it impossible to even touch the fringes of this extensive category. This chapter will attempt to examine the various models of each with regards to pricing and grading.

In the realm of baseballs, highly collectible would be the official Federal, Negro, American, and National League balls, as well as early lemon peel models. In addition there are early figure eights, minor leagues, picture boxes, facsimile autographs (both individual and by team), yellow night baseballs, generic baseballs with graphic boxes, early non-official balls, playground balls, softballs, and so on.

Official American Football League and white Dukes are highly sought footballs as are rugby style footballs from the turn of the century. Official Dukes, Spalding J5-V models, facsimile autograph models, both individual and team, are also collected.

Official American Basketball Association basketballs are highly collectible as are the old laced varieties. Endorsed models also exist. As the popularity of basketball increases, so too, will the demand for basketball equipment.

Collecting the various balls has become something of a passion in itself. There are several known collectors specializing in this field alone.

BASEBALLS

The following notes on the baseball come from the Hall of Fame.

Early days - Earliest examples had lead centers wrapped in twine and covered with chamois or sheepskin. Lead was replaced by strips of rubber rolled into a ball and covered as above. The strips were later replaced by melted rubber. The total weight of a finished ball was 3 ozs. Various leather coverings were introduced such as the lemon peel, half moon, and belt balls. Hand stitched.

1854 - Weight increased to 5-1/2 ozs. Circumference 8-5/8-11".

1856-71 - Weight and circumference, respectively, changed from 5 ozs. to 6-1/4 ozs. and from 9" to 10-1/4".

1860s - The figure 8 ball or cover introduced, much the same as is used today. Patented by Harwood of Natick, Massachusetts, and designed by C.H. Jackson.

1870 - Dead ball introduced due to high scores.

The Official American Association Ball

Adopted by the AMERICAN ASSOCIATION for 5 Years

Is of the **Same Quality** in every respect as the **American League Ball**

ABSOLUTELY GUARANTEED

No. 1	-	-	Each	-	-	**$ 1.25**
CLUB PRICE	-	-	Per Dozen	-	-	**$15.00**

Patent and registry applied for

18

Example of The Reach Official American Association Baseball as advertised in the Reach Baseball Goods Catalog 1909 Season.

1871 - Rubber center restricted to 1 oz.

1874 - Weight and size must be indicated on cover to be used in official game.

1877 - All balls must be supplied by Secretary of the League.

1879 - Spalding ball designated as official ball of the National League made with black stitching.

1882 - Mahn ball (the double ball or ball within a ball) designated as official ball of the American Association.

1883-91 - Reach ball replaced Mahn ball.

1884 - Wright & Ditson ball designated official ball of the Union Association.

1886 - Plastic cement replaces double cover.

1890 - Keefe & Becannon's designated official ball of the Players League.

1901 - Reach ball designated first official ball of the newly formed American League. Made with red & blue stitching.

1904 - Facsimile autograph of National League President Pulliam stamped on all official National League balls.

1911 - Red & black stitching replaces black stitching on National League balls.

1914-15 - Victor is designated official ball of the newly formed Federal League.

1920 - Balls no longer have gloss.

1925 - Cork center introduced.

1934 - Red stitching replaces the alternate colored stitching of both the National League and American League baseballs.

1938-39 - Yellow baseballs used by Brooklyn.

1970 - Orange baseballs used in spring training.

1974 - Cowhide replaces horsehide as covering.

1977 - Rawlings ball designated official ball of both leagues.

1992 - Blue and orange stitching used for balls in All-Star game at San Diego, California.

Official Brands Of Major League Baseball And The League Presidents

LEAGUE	YEARS	BRAND (STITCHING COLOR)
American	1901-33	Reach (red & blue)
	1934-74	Reach (red)
	1975-76	Spalding (red)
	1977-present	Rawlings (red)
National	1876-77	No official ball
	1878-1910	Spalding (black)
	1911-33	Spalding (red & black)

	1934-77	Spalding (red)
	1978-present	Rawlings (red)
Federal	1914-15	Victor
American Assoc.	1882	Mahn
	1883-91	Reach
Players Assoc.	1890	Keefe & Becannon's
Union Assoc.	1884	Wright & Ditson

20th Century League Presidents

National League

1902-July 29, 1909	Harry Pulliam
July 30-Dec. 15, 1909	John Heydler
1909-1913	Thomas Lynch
1913-1918	John Tener
1918-1934	John Heydler
1934-1951	Ford Frick
1951-1969	Warren Giles
1970-1986	Charles Feeney
1987-1989	Bartlett Giamatti
1989-	William White

American League

1901-1927	Ban Johnson
1927-1931	Ernest Barnard
1931-1959	William Harridge
1959-1973	Joe Cronin
1974-1983	Lee Macphail
1984-	Robert Brown

Negro Leagues - There were so many leagues that a complete list is impossible. Official balls made by Wilson and Rawlings have been examined. They bore the name of League President J.B. Martin. Any official Negro League ball would be collectible.

Glossary

Generic balls - i.e., not official league balls; many nineteenth century balls are stamped with names such as Champion, Cock of the Walk, Union, etc., and are collectible.

Minor League - Refers to such leagues as the Pacific Coast League (PCL), International League, etc.

WILSON EQUIPMENT FOR THE GAME OF DIAMOND BALL

BALLS

 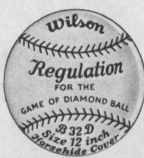

B112D. 12-inch Official Ball for the Game of Diamond Ball. Made of compressed long fibre kapok center, wound with wool yarn, covered with finest selection pearl grain horsehide, double stitched regular inseam sewed....................Each, $1.50

B32D. 12-inch Regulation Ball, for the Game of Diamond Ball, regular inseam sewed; special compressed long fibre kapok center wound with wool yarn; covered with good grade pearl grain horsehide.....................................Each, $1.25

BATS

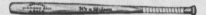

A34. Official Bat—especially designed for the Game of Diamond Ball; dark walnut finish; taped handle. Ea. $1.25

GLOVES AND MITTS

 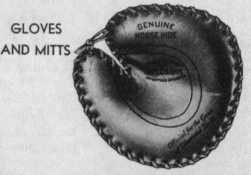

674. Fielders' Glove, especially designed for the Game of Diamond Ball; large pattern, selected tan horsehide, leather welted seams, lightly padded heel and little finger; circular stitched palm; leather laced heel.....................................Each, $3.50

676. Fielders' Glove, especially designed for the Game of Diamond Ball; medium size tan horsehide, leather welted seams, lightly padded heel and little finger, circular stitched palm; leather laced heel.
Each, $3.00

548. Catchers' Mitt, especially designed for the Game of Diamond Ball; selected horsehide, tan color full laced edge, special felt pad, with large pocket; circular stitched palm.....................Each, $4.00

MASKS

W355. Catchers' Mask, especially suitable for the Game of Diamond Ball, electrically welded metal frame, leather pads filled with curled hair.
Each, $3.00

7

Ad for Wilson Equipment for the Game of Diamond Ball from the Wilson Athletic Equipment Spring & Summer 1932 Catalog. Note the baseballs' pricetags of $1.50 and $1.25.

*Trophy ball with two-toned shell and tight stitch marked 5-3 AMHERST
May 5, 1888.*

*Early lemon peel on left with a cricket ball on right for comparison. Lemon
peels ca. 1860-70.*

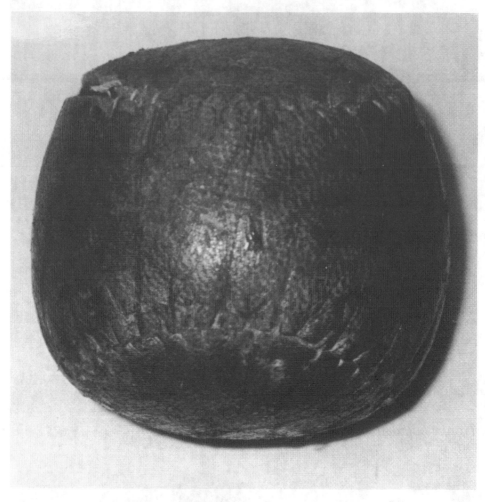

Early figure 8 baseball ca. 1870-80s.

BASE BALL

Spalding's 'Varsity League Ball

Regulation size and weight, fine selected horsehide cover, rubber centre, all wool yarn and far superior in material and workmanship to any of the various imitations of our Official League Ball. Warranted to last a full game without losing its elasticity or shape.

No. **X**. Each, **$1.00**

The Spalding Official Boys' League Ball

Combining all the excellent qualities of our National League Ball, and is carefully made in every particular. It is especially designed for junior clubs (composed of boys under sixteen years of age), and all games in which this ball is used will be recognized as legal games, the same as if played with the Official League Ball. Each ball put up in separate box and sealed, and warranted to last a full game.

No **1B**. Each, **75c.**

Spalding's Interscholastic League Ball

Same quality as the 'Varsity League, but smaller in size. Each ball in sealed box and warranted to last a full game.

No **XB**. Each, **50c.**

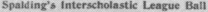

Spalding's Double Seam Ball	Spalding's Professional Ball

Spalding's Double Seam Ball

Made with the same care and of the same material as our League Ball; the double stitch is used in its construction, rendering it doubly secure against ripping. Every ball is wrapped in tinfoil, packed in a separate box and sealed, and warranted to last a full game.

No. **O.** Each, **$1.25**

Spalding's Professional Ball

Full size ball. Made of carefully selected material throughout, and warranted first-class quality. Each ball put up in a separate box and sealed.

No **2.** Each, **50c.**

Spalding's Amateur Ball

Full size ball. Selected horsehide cover, and well adapted for practice games. Each ball put up in a separate box and sealed.

No. **3.** Each, **50c.**

Spalding's King of the Diamond

This ball is full size, made of good material and horsehide cover. Each ball put up in a separate box and sealed.

No. **5.** Each, **25c.**

Three requisites of a perfect base ball—roundness, elasticity, and the Spalding trade-mark.

4

Baseballs for sale in the A.G. Spalding & Brothers 1904 Spring/Summer Catalog.

Lemon peel - Early, pre-1880 baseball in which the leather covering has sections, usually four, that peel like a slice of lemon.

Figure 8 - Two figure 8 pieces of leather sewn together, the same style as used today.

Sweet spot - Term used for spot on a figure 8 ball where the leather narrows or comes together at its closest point. There are two sweet spots to each ball. One will have the factory stamping i.e., league, maker, etc. The other will be left blank.

Belt ball - Hand stitched around center of ball, ca. pre-1880.

Autograph model - Refers to the facsimile autograph of a famous player stamped on the ball.

To find the baseballs in their original boxes is not uncommon and that is the condition most desired. Early baseballs such as the lemon peel or belt ball are all but impossible to find in an original box.

Grading

Fair/Poor - Stitching torn, markings illegible, heavy scuffing and staining, stuffing visible.

Good - Stitching loose, markings barely visible, scuffing and staining, complete.

Very Good - Stitching intact, markings visible, light scuffing and staining, complete.

Excellent - Markings easily read, exhibit minimal use, no stains but some fading, stitching complete and tight.

Near Mint - Shows only the minutest use or storage marks. A few slight dark spots, maybe a bat mark, but almost as taken from box. Slight toning or yellowing.

Mint - No use at all, markings strong, no fading or toning of any kind. No storage marks. Baseballs in this condition are usually found with their original box.

Mint In Box - Exactly that, seal intact and unopened. If box is opened but ball is mint, then it must be listed as follows: a mint ball with its original box but opened. To be considered truly mint in box, it cannot be opened or have the seal removed.

Price Guide

Listed prices are for early balls in the V.G., EXC. and NR/MT categories. Balls of the twentieth century will be priced in the EXC., NR/MT and MIB category. Balls that are mint but without boxes, or ones that are opened, would fall between the last two categories.

It is assumed that boxes have only minor shelf wear. If heavily soiled or damaged, it would lessen the boxed value.

TYPE	V.G.	EXC.	NR/MT	SUPPLY
Lemon peel	$350	$500	$1000	common
Belt ball	$200	$400	$600	rare
Any other hand stitched early baseballs or variations of the above	$150	$300	$450	varies
Pre-1900 generic	$100	$200	$300	varies
Players League	$400	$800	$1200	rare
Union Assoc.	$400	$800	$1200	rare
American Assoc.	$400	$800	$1200	rare

Add 50% to above prices for mint specimens. At least that if boxed.

TWENTIETH CENTURY	EXC.	NR/MT	MIB	SUPPLY
National League				
Harry Pulliam	$400	$800	$1200	rare
T.J. Lynch	$400	$800	$1200	rare
John Tenor	$400	$800	$1200	rare
John Heydler	$300	$600	$900	rare
Ford Frick	$100	$200	$300	common
Warren Giles	$50	$75	$150	common
Charles Feeney	$25	$50	$75	common
Bart Giamatti	$10	$20	$30	common
American League				
Ban Johnson	$400	$800	$1200	rare
Ernest Barnard	$300	$600	$900	rare
William Harridge				
Red & blue stitch	$150	$250	$350	rare
Red stitch	$100	$200	$300	common
Joe Cronin	$50	$75	$150	common
Lee Macphail	$25	$50	$75	common
Federal League	$500	$1000	$1500	rare
Negro League	$400	$800	$1200	rare
Yellow official ball	$400	$800	$1200	rare
Generic				
Multi color stitch	$100	$200	$300	varies

One color stitch	$25	$50	$75	varies

Triple A Minor League
balls such as PCL, Inter-

national League, etc.	$50	$75	$150	varies

Facsimile Autograph Models

Prewar Hofers	$75	$100	$200	varies
Prewar stars	$50	$75	$150	varies
Postwar Hofers	$20	$40	$125	varies
Postwar stars	$15	$30	$100	varies

Prices listed above as MIB (mint in box) are for boxes that picture a player. If it is an endorsement model and the box is sealed and there is no picture, it would be worth 20% less.

FOOTBALLS

In 1869, in a game between Princeton and Rutgers, football was played with a round English soccer ball. In 1874, the Rugby style ball was adopted for football. Originally played only with the feet, rugby introduced the use of hands in 1823 but the ball could not be passed forward until 1906. It was a rule that remained untested until Gus Dorais and Knute Rockne of Notre Dame became regular practitioners.

Football weights and shapes changed little throughout the first decades of the twentieth century. The dimensions of ll-11-1/4" set in 1931 and 12-1/2- 13-1/2 air pounds set in 1934 remains the same today.

Air stems used to fill the balls resembled automobile stems and were first filled by players blowing air into them and tucking the stem inside, then relacing. The stem was later made of rubber and in 1886, Peck & Snyder developed "The New Patent Foot Ball Inflator", a pump that could fill a ball to capacity in five minutes.

Prelacing, and allowing the ball to be filled through a hole in the ball in which an air stem was placed, was introduced in 1920.

White footballs were introduced to the NFL in 1956 and lasted a few years. The white lines on footballs, also used for night play, were banned in 1976 since when wet, they made the ball too slick to handle.

Numerous companies made footballs stamped with famous players' names and Wilson even made footballs with stamped autographs of entire teams. There are child, rubber, and plastic models as well, but they are generally not collectible.

Official Footballs

1920-1940	Spalding J5-V, also used by the AFL from 1960-1969.
1941-1969	Wilson Duke Official League
1970-	NFL

Spalding J5-V white football. This was the official NFL ball from 1920s through 1940 when the Duke ball was adopted. This white ball was used at dusk and was intended for college play.

Early pre-bladder rugby style football ca. 1890-1910.

OFFICIAL INTERCOLLEGIATE

Wilson KR

FOOTBALL

Equipped
With the
New
PATENTED
PERFECTED
EVEN-CONTOUR
WILSON VALVE

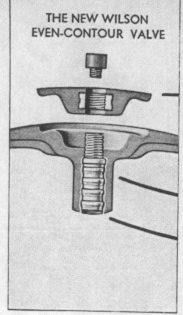

THE NEW WILSON
EVEN-CONTOUR VALVE

KR. The Wilson-Rockne Official Intercollegiate Football, perfected under the direction of the famous Notre Dame Coach, Knute K. Rockne.

It is the original perfected valve type, ready laced football, has become known as "The Perfect Football" because of its perfect shape, balance and liveliness. It has become the choice of leading coaches and universities because of these great features and its proven superiority over the unlined type of ball. It is a livelier ball and holds its shape because of the patented double lining. The Rockne double lace insures a firmer grip in passing and is the only lacing which double locks and permanently closes the lacing aperture. Made of finest selected specially tanned pebble grain cowhide. Comes to you already laced and ready for instant inflation without disturbing lacing. Complete with Wilson patented valve bladder......................Each, $14.00

WILSON OFFICIAL FOOTBALL

A5V. Wilson Official Intercollegiate double laced, double lined valve type football.....................Each, $14.00

92

Example of the Wilson-Rockne Official Intercollegiate Football "perfected under the direction of the famous Notre Dame Coach, Knute K. Rockne." From the Wilson 1932 Spring & Summer Athletic Equipment Catalog.

GoldSmith *All-America* Sport Sets

No. SP40 — "All - America" Football, Helmet, and Shoulder Pad Set. Consists of regulation size football, juvenile helmet, and juvenile shoulder pad.
Per Set, $5.50

No. SP40

No. SP80 — "All-America" Basketball and Goal Set. Consists of regulation size basketball, and one goal with net.
Per Set, $3.75

No. SP80

No. SP20 — "All-America" Football and Helmet Set. Consists of regulation size football, and juvenile helmet.
Per Set, $3.50

No. SP20

No. SP100 "All-America" Striking Bag and Platform Set. Consists of valve type striking bag, and striking bag platform.
Per Set, $4.50

No. SP100

— 91 —

Examples of Sport Sets for Sale in the Goldsmith Sports Equipment 1942 Spring & Summer Catalog.

Glossary

Bladder - The rubber insides of a football.

Rugby style - More rounded than today's football.

Bladder ball - Term used to describe pre-1920 ball in which there is no outside air hole for inflation. Bladder must be blown up in another manner, then the ball must be relaced.

Pebble grain - The texture of the football used by the NFL today.

Smooth model - Exactly that, no texture, smooth leather.

Grading

Fair/Poor - No longer holds air, major tears or holes, dry rot, heavy soiling and wear. Bladder rotten or missing. Markings gone.

Good - Complete without holes or dry rot but doesn't hold air. Heavy wear, markings light but mostly legible.

Very Good - Complete and holds air for a short time. Markings clear, heavy wear.

Excellent - Holds air, complete, all markings clear, light wear and scuffing.

Near Mint - Used little with only minor scuffing.

Mint - Not used, often found in original bags or generic boxes.
Add 50% for official balls, 25% on others.

Price Guide

TYPE	V.G.	EXC.	NR/MT	SUPPLY
Bladder ball	$100	$200	$300	rare
AFL ball	$100	$200	$300	common
White Duke	$200	$400	$600	rare
Spalding J5-V	$75	$150	$200	common
NFL Duke	$75	$150	$200	common
Endorsed Models Prewar Hall of Fame	$50	$75	$150	varies

Stars	$40	$60	$120	varies
Teams	$100	$200	$300	varies
Postwar				
Hall of Fame	$25	$50	$75	varies
Stars	$20	$40	$60	varies
Teams	$50	$75	$150	varies

The above prices on endorsed models are for stamped signatures as they were available from a store. Hand autographed models would be worth much more. Picture boxes of endorsed footballs are collectible and would add at least 100% to any model.

BASKETBALLS

Not highly sought until just recently, there are really only a few collectible categories. Grading would be the same as the footballs. Prices for boxes with pictures would be on par with footballs as well. Laced basketballs have a lacing system similar to footballs and were popular until the 1950s. American Basketball Association balls are the most highly coveted, followed by laced models, early NBA balls, and prewar Hall of Fame stamped models. Watch for increased interest as basketball becomes more popular and older stars hit the autograph and show circuit. Also watch for early basketballs with nice early makers stamps.

Price Guide

TYPE	V.G.	EXC.	NR/MT	SUPPLY
ABA	$100	$200	$300	rare
NBA (early)	$50	$75	$150	varies
Laced	$50	$75	$150	common
Stamped, (early)	$50	$75	$150	varies
ENDORSED				
Prewar				
Hall of Fame	$50	$75	$150	varies
Stars	$40	$80	$120	varies
Postwar				
Hall of Fame	$40	$80	$120	varies
Stars	$20	$40	$60	varies

Group of four assorted early laced basketballs showing different seams and styles.

Basketballs and basketball bladders advertised in the Elliott 1931 Fall & Winter Sports Catalog No.56.

MISCELLANEOUS EQUIPMENT

Epuipment:
  Hockey
  Basketball
Other:
  Letterman Sweaters
  Striped Socks

HOCKEY EQUIPMENT

This is an area that offers lots of possibilities for beginning collectors. Old jerseys, pucks, sticks, goalies' gear, skates–all are collectible but there doesn't seem to be a lot of older stuff out there. Early jerseys are basically the same as football jerseys, resembling heavy sweaters with stripes on the arms or across the body. Skates with pictures of famous players on the box are collectible, yet other skates, sans boxes, have little value.

Early goalies' masks, made from resin, are extremely scarce as are the leather goalies' pads from the 1920s and 1930s. Both are wanted for displays. Strap helmets survive in fairly good supplies. Sticks from the 1930s and earlier with their original paper labels are scarce, as are the early pucks with the team logos on them. Hockey knickers dating from the late 1890s look so much like quilted football pants that unless they have a Canadian label, you will probably not be able to tell the difference. Following is a list of the most desirable items and some price ranges.

Price Guide

Skates - Unless in original picture box, they have little value.
Prices given for boxes in nice shape with skates intact.

Prewar Hall of Fame	$400-500
Prewar stars	$200-300
Postwar Hall of Fame	$100-200
Postwar stars	$50-100
Resin goalie masks, ca. 1940s	$400-500
Strap helmets ca. 1950s	$100-150
Sticks, pre-1940 with paper labels intact	$100-150
Jerseys	$200-300
Pucks, early models with old National Hockey League logos intact	$25-50
Obsolete NHL teams	$50-100
Quilted hockey knickers	$150-250

Early quilted goalie pads,
complete $100-150
As above, but all leather $150-200

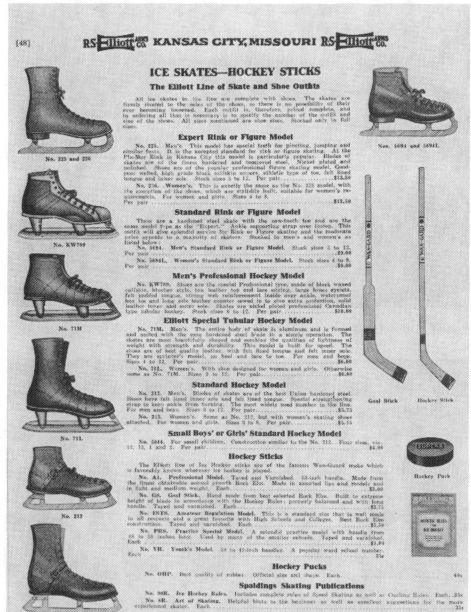

Hockey equipment for sale in the Elliott 1931 Fall & Winter Sports Catalog No. 56

Boxed Bobby Orr signature skates ca. 1960s.

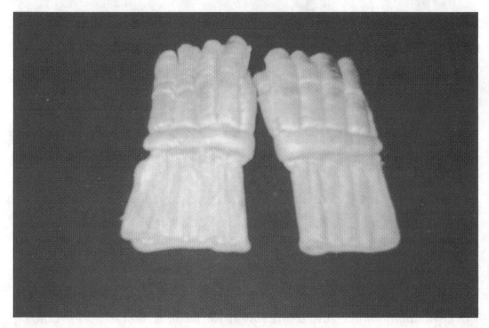

Leather goalie gloves ca. 1940-50.

A nice closeup of detail on early all-leather hockey goalie pads.

Various basketball equipment for sale in the A.G. Spalding & Brothers 1904 Spring/Summer Catalog.

WILSON BASKETBALL SHOES

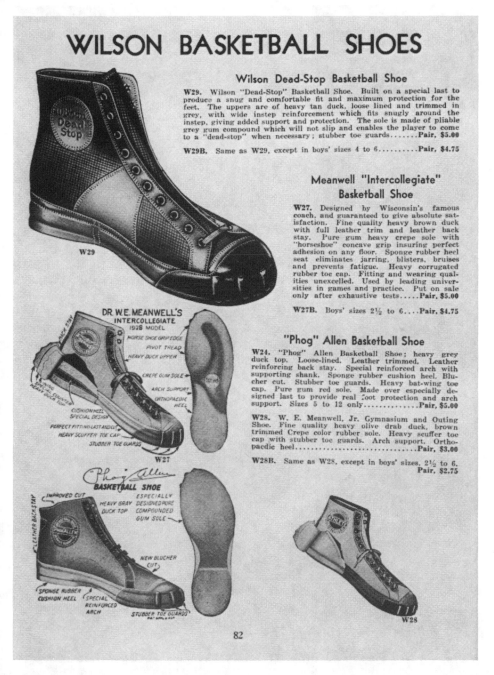

Wilson Dead-Stop Basketball Shoe

W29. Wilson "Dead-Stop" Basketball Shoe. Built on a special last to produce a snug and comfortable fit and maximum protection for the feet. The uppers are of heavy tan duck, loose lined and trimmed in grey, with wide instep reinforcement which fits snugly around the instep, giving added support and protection. The sole is made of pliable grey gum compound which will not slip and enables the player to come to a "dead-stop" when necessary; stubber toe guards........**Pair, $5.00**

W29B. Same as W29, except in boys' sizes 4 to 6..........**Pair, $4.75**

Meanwell "Intercollegiate" Basketball Shoe

W27. Designed by Wisconsin's famous coach, and guaranteed to give absolute satisfaction. Fine quality heavy brown duck with full leather trim and leather back stay. Pure gum heavy crepe sole with "horseshoe" concave grip insuring perfect adhesion on any floor. Sponge rubber heel seat eliminates jarring, blisters, bruises and prevents fatigue. Heavy corrugated rubber toe cap. Fitting and wearing qualities unexcelled. Used by leading universities in games and practice. Put on sale only after exhaustive tests.....**Pair, $5.00**

W27B. Boys' sizes 2½ to 6....**Pair, $4.75**

"Phog" Allen Basketball Shoe

W24. "Phog" Allen Basketball Shoe; heavy grey duck top. Loose-lined. Leather trimmed. Leather reinforcing back stay. Special reinforced arch with supporting shank. Sponge rubber cushion heel. Blucher cut. Stubber toe guards. Heavy bat-wing toe cap. Pure gum red sole. Made over especially designed last to provide real foot protection and arch support. Sizes 5 to 12 only..............**Pair, $5.00**

W28. W. E. Meanwell, Jr. Gymnasium and Outing Shoe. Fine quality heavy olive drab duck, brown trimmed Crepe color rubber sole. Heavy scuffer toe cap with stubber toe guards. Arch support. Orthopaedic heel...............................**Pair, $3.00**

W28B. Same as W28, except in boys' sizes, 2½ to 6.
Pair, $2.75

82

Basketball shoes as advertised in the Wilson Athletic Equipment 1932 Spring & Summer Catalog.

Nice basketball display with early laced ball, trophies, pennants, high-top shoes, knee pads, and basketball ad. While college pennants, knee pads, and high top sneakers don't add much value to a collection, they artistically improve displays and can be purchased rather inexpensively.

BASKETBALL EQUIPMENT

Much like hockey, basketball equipment is beginning to find interested collectors, but there doesn't appear to be much out there. Old generic jerseys and trunks command little collector interest. The wire face mask that covers only the eyes and was invented to protect eyeglasses, and one that is often mistaken for a catcher's mask, also commands little attention. Early sneakers, if mint in the box and bearing a picture of a famous player on the cover, have respectable value. In addition to the old basketballs, there is little else, equipment related, to collect. The following list covers most of what is available.

Price Guide

Old wool jerseys and shorts (set)	$25-50
Eyeglass mask (wire)	$25-50
Shoes in picture boxes Pre-1960	
Hall of Fame	$150-200
Stars	$100-150
Post-1960	
Hall of Fame	$100-150
Stars	$50-100

Deduct 50% for any shoes size 8 or less.

LETTERMAN SWEATERS

These heavy-wool sweaters were made in pull-over, button-down and/or cowl neck styles from the 1890s-1920s. Since these sweaters were sometimes worn by teams and also by others at various colleges, they cannot be called jerseys. Sweaters bearing numbers on the front would have been used in team sports and would have at least 50% higher values. Famous Ivy League schools such as Harvard or Princeton would also bring a 20-40% premium.

Price Guide

VALUES	VERY GOOD	EXCELLENT	NEAR-MINT
	$100	$200	$300

Pullover sweater with numbers on front, indicating sports use.

Pullover sweater with "P" (Princeton?).

Pullover sweater with "I" and sleeve stripe on one sleeve.

Pullover sweater with "C" on front.

College letterman's sweater with rubber noseguard under an original team photograph showing players wearing letter sweaters. (Note the same one.) Appears to be turn of the century college football team.

SOCKS

Socks are not really collected and have little or no value on their own. However, they go great with uniform displays. Early all-wool striped socks were worn for both football and baseball.

Striped socks–Early all-wool striped football and baseball socks. Not really collected and have little or no value on their own, but these items go great with early uniform displays.

Front and back covers of a 1922 D & M catalog.

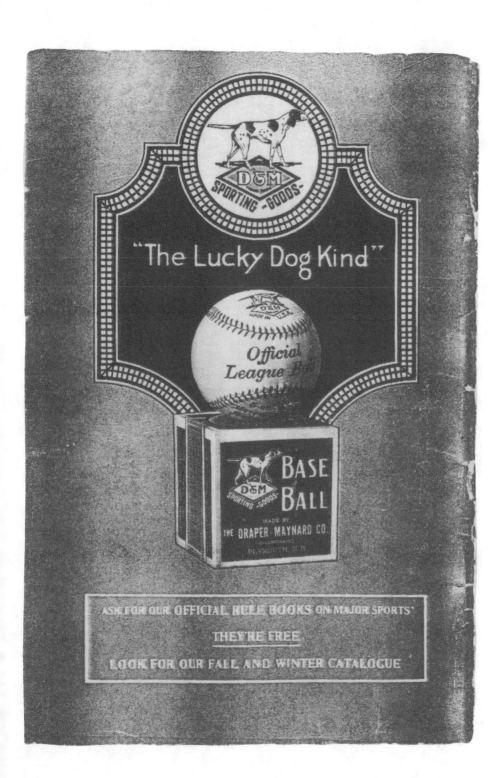

WILSON ATHLETIC STOCKINGS

Jersey Knit Football Hose	Jersey Knit Basketball Hose	Sanitary Stockings	Athletic Socks

JERSEY KNIT FOOTBALL HOSE

Fine quality pure worsted; footless only. Special to order only; ten-day delivery in any of our solid standard colors.

C195. Extra Heavy Weight.............Pair, $3.00
C197. Medium Heavy Weight...........Pair, 2.25

JERSEY KNIT BASKETBALL HOSE

Fine quality pure worsted, calf length, footless only; special to order only, ten-day delivery in any of our solid standard colors.

C220. Heavy weight....................Pair, $2.00
C217. Medium weight...................Pair, 1.60

SANITARY STOCKINGS

C555. Full length white, to be worn under colored footless style stockings...................Pair, $0.25

ATHLETIC SOCKS

C553. Wool mixed heavy weight ankle length socks.
Pair, $0.50
C552. Made of 100% wool yarn. Medium weight ankle length............................Pair, $0.75
C556. Cotton, ankle length socks........Pair, $0.40
C554. Wool mixed ankle length socks. Fancy knit tops....................................Pair, $1.00

Tops on C554 supplied either in solid colors or striped. C554 made to order only.

WILSON ATHLETIC SUPPORTERS

B386	B388	B389	A370	B385	B383

B386. Wilson Combination Supporter and Abdominal Protector. Elastic Supporter with three-inch waist and leg bands, with special elastic pouch into which is fitted a moulded aluminum form-fitting protector, affording the maximum in supporter protection..Each, $2.50

B387. Elastic Supporter with pouch only, without aluminum protector.......................Each, $ .90

B388. Wilson Moulded Aluminum Protector only for use with B387 or similar type supporter..Each, $1.60

B389. Wilson Moulded Aluminum Protector with foam rubber edging........................Each, $2.25

A370. Wilson Aluminum Abdominal Protector. Well padded at edges. To be worn with any supporter. Complete with elastic cross bands and belt..Each, $4.00

B385. Wilson Special Athletic Supporter and Abdominal band combined. All elastic 6-inch waist-band with 2-inch leg straps. Wide waist-band gives additional support to abdomen................Each, $0.75

B383. Wilson "All-Elastic" Supporter. Made from specially woven fabric of Egyptian yarn and best para rubber..Each, $0.50

B381. Athletic Supporter. Good quality elastic waist-band and leg straps. Non-elastic mesh pouch.
Each, $0.50

B378. Genuine "Bike" All-elastic Supporter. Made of best Egyptian yarn and para rubber....Each, $0.50

38

Athletic stockings and supporters as advertised in the Wilson Athletic Equipment 1932 Spring & Summer Catalog.

'UNSER CHOE' HAUSER:

Home Run King
of the Minor Leagues

(In 1992 David Bushing conducted an interview with Joe "Unser Choe" Hauser, a baseball player who made his mark both in the major and minor leagues. Hauser's recollection of his playing days offers an insider's view to the sports equipment used during a bygone era of our national pastime.)

Mention home run king to a sports fan and the response may be as varied as the person you're asking. Single season or lifetime? Did Maris really break Ruth's record or should the asterisk remain? Will anyone ever get close to Aaron? Old National League fans might even bring Hack Wilson into the discussion, but one name that usually draws a blank expression when mentioned within the realm of home run kings is Joe "Unser Choe" Hauser.

Who? you might ask. Well, if you're an old-time baseball fanatic it's a name you should know because he played six seasons in the majors, five of them under Connie Mack. But what he's really remembered for is his record-setting season with the Minneapolis Millers in 1933, a year he belted 69 roundtrippers to set a record that would stand until it was tied in 1948 by Bob Crues of Amarillo and finally broken in 1954 by Joe Bauman of the Roswell Rockets with 72 homers, a record that still stands.

When I found out from Ray Berres, the great White Sox pitching coach, that Unser Choe lived less than two hours from me, in Sheboygan, Wisconsin, I called information and got his number and address and dropped him a line. Two weeks later I found a hand-written note addressed from Joe. It read on the back, "bring cigars." A quick call to set up the time and the next week found me at his door, a box of Antonio & Cleopatra's tucked under one arm, an old Joe Hauser game bat, a left-handed first base mitt circa 1920, an old baseball and a briefcase full of interview essentials under the other. Although 93 years old, he still lives on the third floor of the old brick apartment house that he has called home for more than 30 years. I knew the minute I walked into the complex that I was in the right place; the smell of cigars permeated down to the lobby.

My knock on his door was met with a thundering response of, "Come on in, the door's open." There, in an old easy chair, sat "Unser Choe," a nickname that apparently in Dutch means "our Joe," the reason for this name I will explain later. He still looked a lot like his pictures from 60 years ago. Although he complains of being off balance as of late, he got up, shook my hand and grabbed his

1924   Best Wishes to Dave   Joe Hauser

old game bat. He hadn't seen one in years, and aside from a few articles and a couple of awards, he had kept nothing from his baseball career. After a couple of swings he quipped, "If it isn't 34 inches, it isn't my bat." Well, we pulled out a tape measure and it was 34 on the dot.

It was only about 30 miles south of this Lake Michigan port city, in another port city named Milwaukee, that Joe Hauser was born in 1899. If you'd like that year put into historical perspective, it was less than a year after the Spanish American War and San Juan Hill, only 34 years since the Civil War ended and 18 years before we entered World War I. In his lifetime he has seen almost every invention we take for granted brought to reality: the automobile, the airplane, radio, phones, electricity, and indoor plumbing, just to name a few. Suffice it to say, he has seen more in one lifetime than any of us ever will, and he played ball with some of the greatest names in baseball history.

Although he didn't play with the Athletics in 1929 when they won the World Series against the Cubs, the 1928 team, the one in which he played first base in 95 games, was almost identical. Jimmie Foxx, who was on the team in 1928, moved into Hauser's position at first in 1929. Max Bishop, Joe Boley, Sammy Hale, Bing Miller, Al Simmons, and Mickey Cochrane were the same starting lineup in both 1928 and 1929. Gone was the other starter from the 1928 season, Tyrus Cobb; Mule Haas taking over in 1929 as starting outfielder.

But again, I'm getting ahead of myself. Hauser's career in baseball began like many others at that time, playing farm ball. They didn't have the scouting system they have today, nor did they have the natural progression that is followed by most of today's players: high school ball, followed by college, followed by the minor league system and then, maybe, the majors. In those early days, a lot of kids only went to school until old enough to help full time on the family farm, an institution that was predominant in our country at the turn of the century.

Hauser quit school after the fifth grade and went to work. He became known around the Milwaukee area as a pretty good stick, and when the war broke out in 1917 he was given the opportunity to play in organized ball or fight. He chose the former and at the age of 18, he signed with the Providence Baseball Club. His first full season was 1918 when he started both as a pitcher and an outfielder, batting .277 that first year.

In 1922, he was brought up as Connie Mack's starting first baseman, hitting only nine home runs in 368 at bats, but finishing the season with a respectable .323 batting average. The top pitcher on that team was "Ace" Eddie Rommel, who posted a 27-13 record with a 3.28 ERA. Still, they finished next to last that season, winning 65 and losing 89. The next season, he almost doubled his number of roundtrippers, hitting 16, and batting .307 for the season. In 1924, his home runs increased to 27, although his average slipped to .288 with the Athletics still placing in the bottom half of the league.

The year 1924 brought baseball great Al Simmons to the Athletics. He, like Hauser, was born and raised in Milwaukee and roomed his first year with Joe. He was remembered by Hauser as being a shy farm boy that wanted to know how to act in the majors—what to do, where to go, what to say—and he trusted his fellow townsperson to show him the ropes, a role Unser Choe took to heart.

Which reminds me, about that nickname, what it means and how it stuck. In the early days of baseball, towns were small; everybody turned out for the local team. If you did poorly, you would be razzed right off the field (maybe some things never change), and Milwaukee had a large Dutch and German popula-

JOE HAUSER
FIRST BASE, PHILADELPHIA AMERICANS

tion. When the hometown crowd would begin to harass Joe, locals who knew him and his family would scream something to the effect, "No, no, Unser Choe," which roughly translates to "That's our Joe." He became such a popular figure in Milwaukee that he could do no wrong and no one would boo him no matter what the error, except maybe an occasional out of towner.

A knee injury in 1925 caused him to sit out the season, replaced at first by Jim Poole. It was also the year that saw Philadelphia rise from the cellar into second place and future Hall of Famers Cochrane, Grove, and Foxx joined the team. In 1926, Hauser came back but not at the starting position, and roomed with then-backup catcher, Jimmie Foxx. When asked about what sort of fellow Foxx was, Joe responded, "The greatest. Quiet, he didn't drink and he had arms like a tree trunk."

The 1927 season started with Hauser back in the minors, never fully recovered from his injury. He came back up as the starter in 1928, hitting only 16 homers with a .260 average. Something else happened to Hauser in 1928, something he blames for ruining his career, and that something was known as Ty Cobb.

Cobb was picked up by Mack in 1928 along with another gentleman who was finishing up a Hall of Fame career, Tris Speaker. Hauser was fond of Speaker and had nothing but good things to say about him, but the mere mention of Cobb's name, even after 60 years, gets Hauser's blood boiling; a string of unprintable adjectives is attached to his personal memory of one of baseball's greatest players and one of the most disliked men ever to put on spikes.

It is well known that even Cobb's own teammates didn't like him; several played with him for years, not even talking to him. Hauser recalled playing Detroit and he's in a slump and Harry Heilmann gets on base and he asks if he's on the slide because of Cobb. Apparently, when Heilmann beat out Cobb for the batting title in 1921, as well as in 1923 and 1927, Cobb never again spoke to him, so fierce a competitor that he could not stand to lose, even to his own teammates. It was Cobb's insistence to show Hauser how to bat correctly that was unnerving him so much that to this day, he feels that is the reason he was traded to Cleveland in 1929 and the subsequent reason for his being sent down to the minors.

He recalled two particular instances with Cobb that are still vivid in his memory. The first incident involved the great Connie Mack. Hauser didn't remember the pitcher, but Mack called to Cobb in the dugout and asked if he thought he could hit this guy. Cobb jumped up and said to Mack, "I can hit anybody," at which Mack, incensed at Cobb's arrogance, turned to Joe and said, "You, Hauser, get in there." Hauser remembered striking out, but it didn't really matter because Mack made a fool of Cobb in front of the whole team.

The other time involved a discussion after a game where Cobb proceeded to tell Hauser all the things he was doing wrong on a bad day. Joe got angry and the two got into a shouting match that lasted until they were the only two left in the clubhouse. Hauser finally left the argument and headed into the shower room where, from behind a wall, Connie Mack's son had been listening to the whole thing. He turned to Hauser and said, "Why the hell didn't you punch the S.O.B.?" after which Hauser responded that he wasn't brought up to be a brawler, but he sure would have lit into him if Cobb would have thrown the first punch.

Joe Hauser, first base
MINNEAPOLIS BASEBALL CLUB, 1933

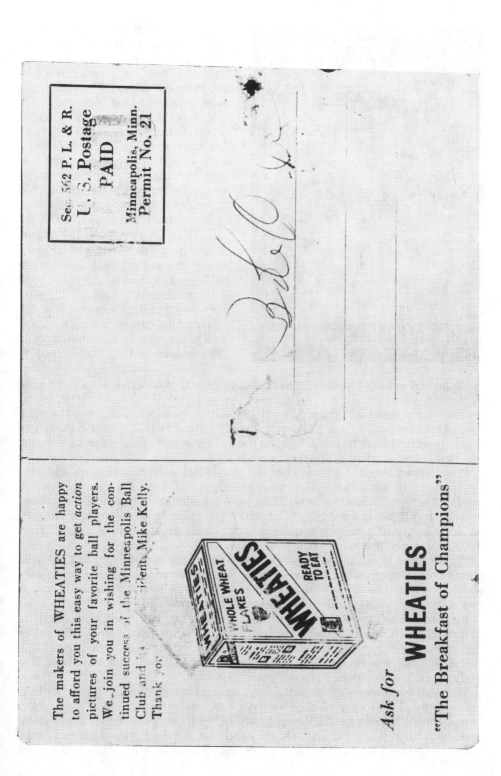

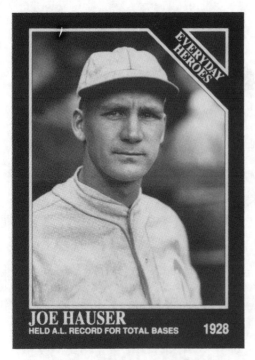

JOE HAUSER
HELD A.L. RECORD FOR TOTAL BASES   1928

The year 1929 found Hauser playing in only 37 games for Cleveland, first base being guarded by Lew Fonseca, who was on his way to a batting title that season. The rest of the team was rounded out with the Sewell brothers, Joe and Luke, future Hall of Famer Earl Averill and Johnny Hodapp and Bib Falk, who both were on their way to .300 seasons. With no place for Hauser to go within the organization and a .250 batting average, he found himself in the International League in 1930.

In 1933, while playing for Minneapolis, he belted his 69 home runs to set the record that stood until 1948. He also holds the distinction of being the only man to hit more than 60 roundtrippers twice in his professional career, hitting 63 home runs while playing with Baltimore in 1930 before setting the record in 1933.

He played with the Millers from 1932-36, was out of baseball until 1940 when he went to Sheboygan as the player-manager from 1940-42. Another short absence from baseball occurred until 1946 when he again was made the manager of Sheboygan, but not a player. It was a position he held until 1951 when he officially retired from baseball to open a sporting goods store in the same town, one that he ran until he sold it in the mid-1970s.

When asked about the Yankees of the mid-1920s, in particular Ruth and Gehrig, Hauser had this to say: "They were the class of the era, it was an honor just to play them at Yankee Stadium. They were a ballclub that could do anything, and Ruth and Gehrig were great. The Babe always had a joke if he ever stopped on first, and Gehrig, he was a quiet guy but had a great sense of humor. They were a class act, that whole ballclub."

When asked about the greatest pitcher he had the opportunity to play with, it was Lefty Grove, "a great pitcher, a hothead that would cuss you out every which way if you blew his lead, and a man with the penchant for a bottle, which you could usually find under his bed, if you were looking."

I had to ask who was the most difficult pitcher he ever faced, and was quite surprised when he answered with Herb Pennock, the great Yankee left-hander. "He threw so many different pitches, you never knew what you'd get," but, Hauser added, "if you were hot, you were hot and you could hit just about anybody; if you were cold, any pitcher could be tough."

With our two-hour visit almost over, I asked Hauser if he'd sign a couple of items for me. I try to get a bat, glove, ball, and card autographed of each player I visit, the collage to be displayed in my office to remember the time I spent with each man. His signature is strong and sharp with a steady hand. I asked about gloves and he said he used a Rawlings left-handed basemitt and a week after our conversation, I came across a 1925 Rawlings catalog showing a Joe Hauser model glove for sale. For the interview, I had a mid-1920s pro model Olympian left-handed basemitt, which he also signed, and an old American League ball. He had several copies of the new Conlon collection card, #548, which he also signed, as well as some reprints of an old postcard from 1924 with him in an A's uniform, which he signed and personalized. According to the stats on the back of the Conlon card, Hauser had a lifetime fielding average of .990, and Joe himself said, "If it came anywhere near first base, I got it. I never let a ball get by me."

My day with the gregarious "Unser Choe" was one of the highlights of life. Humorous, sharp, and witty at 93 with the memories of a lifetime, an enviable thing indeed. He made a living doing what he loved and played with the greatest ballplayers of all time. He was elected to the Wisconsin Hall of Fame in 1967 and given the title, "Home Run King of the Minors." A large photo of him hangs in the Milwaukee Auditorium, and he will be forever remembered in his hometown, a local hero, and in the record books and hearts of his fans for posterity. To many people in Milwaukee and the country, he will always be "Our Joe."

BIBLIOGRAPHY

Diamond, Dan and Romain, Joseph. *Hockey Hall of Fame*. Toronto: Double-day, 1988.

Riffenburgh, Beau. *The Official NFL Encyclopedia*. New York: Times, 1986.

Spalding, A.G. *Base Ball, America's National Game*. San Francisco: Halo, 1915, 1991.

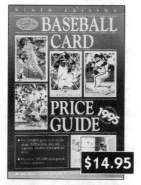

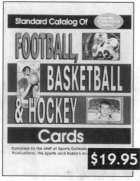

MORE GREAT BOOKS
FOR COLLECTORS

Standard Catalog of Baseball Cards
4th edition

Sportscard Counterfeit Detector
3rd edition

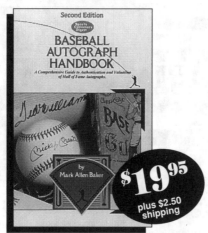

Baseball Autograph Handbook
2nd edition

Complete Guide to Baseball Memorabilia
2nd edition